THIS PESTILENCE,
BERGEN-BELSEN

THIS PESTILENCE, BERGEN-BELSEN

Nigel Clayton

This Pestilence, Bergen-Belsen.
ISBN 978 0 6452 540 7 5

BISAC
HIS043000   HISTORY / Holocaust
HIS027100   HISTORY / Military / World War II
HIS014000   HISTORY / Europe / Germany

IN MEMORY

For my grandfather, James Edward Kelly, died on the 13th day of June, 2008, never having forgotten those thousands that died before him.

He served during World War II, with the Royal West Kent and the Military Police. He served in Europe and was one of the first to step foot into Bergen-Belsen on its liberation. He never spoke of the concentration camp, until lying upon his death bed, and he was more than adamant about one thing, and that was of the atrocities that Germany's Third Reich had committed.

The holocaust was real, and he was angered by all of those that claimed it to be nothing more than a lie, saying that it never happened: it did, and his last message for us all, before he died, was for us not to forget the holocaust or camps similar to Bergen-Belsen.

Epic poems by this author:

Afghan - Song of the Desert
Orcinus Orca - Song of the Ocean
Hollandia Nova - Song of the Coast
Kibeho - An Epic Poem
Song of the Templar [poetic verse]
Songs of Australia - A Poetic Trilogy
1453 - Constantinople

Other titles by this author:

The Long Road to Rwanda
The Templar: and the City of God [Part 1]
The Templar: and the Temple of Káros [Part 2]
The Templar: and the Cross of Christ [Part 3]
Amazon [Part 4 of The Templar series]
Chivalry [Omnibus]
Underworld
Templar, Assassination, Trial & Torture
Dreamtime - An Aboriginal Odyssey
The Zuytdorp Survivors
Afghan Camel Strings and the Australian Outback
Tom of Twofold Bay
This Pestilence, Bergen-Belsen
When the Virgin Falls
Afghan: The Script
Colonies of Earth: also known as Mildratawa
Fall of the Inca Empire
Kibeho: Original Script
The Kibeho Massacre: As It Happened
Furious George

PROLOGUE

Bergen-Belsen was initially a Prisoner of War and concentration camp of specific need, that need being to provide a place in which to house allied Prisoners of War and to fill an exchange quota designed to release German Prisoners of War of their shackles. This was to be organised and carried out by exchanging imprisoned Jews for German Prisoners of War held by the allies. It came to pass, however, that in the few months before the end of the war – due to an overwhelming allied advance, in particular from the East – an injection of prisoners completely inundated the camp to such a degree that it would become the pestilence of humanity, a thorn in the side of the Nazi Regime, a sickening episode in our history that cannot be explained in simple words or terms. It was a disease, an epidemic, a plague; all of this and much, much more; the Third Reich was responsible; it had single-handedly created this disaster through the habits of its cruelty.

By April, 1945, there were 60,000 prisoners housed in a camp built for no more than 10,000 and the camp as a whole was divided into sections, comprising camps for women, Hungarians, and Prisoners of War; there were also sections labelled 'star' (which comprised mostly of Dutch Jews), 'special', 'neutral', and a tent camp, which comprised mostly of Polish women from Auschwitz. It was testament to Hitler's viciousness.

The camp was liberated by the British on 15th April, 1945, and over the next 30 days the death rate dropped from 500 a day to less than 100 a day. More and more people continued to meet with death in the face of their liberation for many reasons, some of which have been needlessly blamed on the British for their heroic efforts. Of all the care and assistance given to those poor wretches, the shining light from heaven above continued to call out to those too poorly to make it through those trying times, and the Golden gates remained open to them all.

The fight to preserve life was a constant battle but one that was often lost. In total around 14,000 of those imprisoned died in the four weeks after their liberation [Which doesn't spell accurately for that would mean 500 deaths per day and via one source - see previous paragraph - I have found advice that the death rate dropped to around 100 per day - I'm sure you can do the math].

On 21st May, a ceremony was held where the last of the memories was purged by flame, symbols of the Nazi Regime, and the last of the huts was torched and burnt to the ground in one huge emotional wave of relief.

The world's Jewish population in 1939 was around 9,242,500 and by the end of the war only 5,447,000 remained. The death toll was staggering to say the least.

The following story is but one of many, which commences in the latter part of 1944, and concludes in May of 1945.

This is a work of historical-fiction, as names and some actions I speak about are not valid and/or may not have happened precisely as written; nevertheless, Bergen-Belsen and the atrocities carried out there are not fictitious and therefore I have labelled this book as being historical: label me as you will.

CHAPTER 1

The female prisoners were from Auschwitz; all Polish, and all Jews; walking ghosts and with nothing more than strips of blanket wrapped around them: which was the best that they could scrounge. This was all they had, all that stood between them and the weather, the vicious cold of December falling upon them without remorse.

The fingers of all in the column were freezing, fingertips almost turning black – regardless, some discolouration was evident – in this, the cold of the winter which had arrived several weeks before; thin and weary to the bone they were, mere skeletons of their former selves, and so miserable; so miserable that the feeling couldn't even be expressed in simple words, couldn't be classed as an emotion or condition, a state or frame of mind. Their misery was too powerful to be expressed in any way. If you couldn't have experienced the suffering then you had no way of understanding it.

They were like animals being herded to slaughter; animals being abused by every single physical and emotional means possible. In fact, these very means of control, so heinously, sadistic and sitting dormant in the minds of men, which had not been seen for so very long, were reinvented in quick-time by the SS. Each and every guard present had his mind cast hard upon his ideas for control of the Jews that fell under his ever watchful eye.

Yes, indeed; say the SS; the Führer must be right.

And the guards watched on, spitting upon those close enough to be spat upon, those stinking Jews, so wretched they were. What did they deserve other than a good, hard and swift, kicking in the arse?

Their heads were shaved, here and there the tell-tale signs of truncheon blows having been delivered, beaten down hard against the skull of these women, enemies of the Third Reich, the pests of Hitler's demented mind, and highly sadistic he was. He was the savour of Germany in all its glory, and with that went all reality from mind, for he was nothing less than an insane leech of blood-sucking temperament, even too low to be considered a cockroach or other vile insect of contemptible worth.

None of the prisoners were adequately clothed, not a whole blanket seen anywhere amongst the column of women as they marched from one pestilence to another, making their way towards Bergen-Belsen and into the arms of the devil, where women guards were as atrocious as their male counterparts.

One of the poor women, Ruth; her mind was so numb from the abuse and mistreatment, so frozen from the cold and the misery of death that followed her every step, that she couldn't distinguish reality from hallucination. She caught a glimpse of the body of a baby in the snow during one of the few rest stops provided the column. She stooped over from her place amongst the masses and looked the baby in the face, its eyes closed and body frozen. It couldn't have been more than a few months old. It looked so peaceful, so fast asleep. As the freezing wind swept past her view she saw a little love in it's face, frozen for all time, a child which should have been cared for and nurtured until fully grown, not discarded like a piece of common garbage, a piece of filth.

The baby reminded her of her own, a young child she had been unfortunately torn from during the early days of Germany's intervention upon her happy days and the blessed glory of her freedom. It reminded her so much of the one that she had lost that she couldn't help but to smile and stretch out her arms in order to pick up the prize that she had found. She would rescue it, if none other would. She'd care for it, give it a home, and take care of it as it grew into a young child, a child that she'd mould into likeness of herself.

She brought the bundle of frozen flesh to her breast and smiled ever-more, cradling it in her arms as though her own, and then the order to 'move along' was given once more. So she stood up and continued with the walking, the cold now abated, for her mind was awash with the gift she had been given by the war that surrounded her. And she continued to smile as she walked along, unable to register the reality of the situation for she was insanely mad.

Other women, too, felt the emotions of the war around them, its prodding hatred coming from every angle, the hatred for the Jews present on every wisp of wind, and Judith, being no different than the others, couldn't forgive the Nazis for what they had done to her and her family. Would she ever see them again; she had no idea? The question was impossible to answer.

A few of Judith's friends had gone missing; missing since morning, killed by the hands of the guards that marched them to death, insisting that the Jews continue to march in accordance with the army regulations of so many paces per minute and with arms swinging as though with gusto; but these ridiculous demands did not last long – just long enough for the guards to have their little laugh.

Yes, her friends were few and far between now, many having strolled from the path of the march, blanketed by their clouded minds; their forgetfulness; the delusion of their wandering dreams. And here they would fall from their way and into death's arms, and others would be provided a bullet to the head for their inability to keep up with the others. It was nothing to a soldier of the infamous SS to shoot first and ask questions later, holding a pistol to a young woman's head, shooting her dead, and then asking with a stupid look upon his face, 'don't you wish you'd kept up, ah; you pile of filth; you piece of stinking shit.'

The Russians were coming and nothing could stop them. The Red Army was advancing at great speed towards Berlin and before them the citizens of Germany were running with their tails between their legs, like the true maggots they were, upon horse and cart, or simply walking beside their collection of worldly possessions. Their furniture was atop carts and carried in hand, food in all its glory within reach of those walking the road from one hell camp and into another. These men, women and children of Germany, were looking down with such great spite upon the thousands of Jews making their way into the arms of death; but not a single one, not even the innocent; such as young children; none at all ever attempted to throw even the most meagre of food portions down to them; not an apple or its core, not a potato, not even a slice of bread. 'Look, mummy,' would be heard from atop a cart. 'That one has a little hair on her head,' and a guard would lash out with the butt of his rifle on seeing the Jew look up at the little girl. 'She's bad, mummy; I don't like that one.'

The SS were exchanged at rest stops where much food [Ha!], water and rest, would be accompanied by another unkind word directed at a Polish Jew as they watched on, the line of women passing the guards by in a continuous move forward... ever forward, on and on and on. 'Get your arms swinging, you stupid, lazy whore. It's no wonder you look like shit. I'll kick you in the arse before I put up with your insolent stare. Now look to your front, you ugly bitch.' It was always the same; always the curses of the SS that could be heard over the wind as it blew across the face of Europe.

And then it was their time to eat, a rest stop for the guilty; for a prisoner could not be innocent, not by any means. In the minds of the SS these women were all guilty, even without a verdict being read, even without prosecution. These bitches were the scum of the earth and Hitler was right to have them dealt with immediately and viciously.

Yes, at last, a rest stop for the ravenous crowd of women forced to march forever on, forced to march until they dropped, and march until they died. And what of their rations: black bread and soup, but the soup was nothing more than meer water.

The pangs of hunger were throttled aside but only for a few minutes, for what they ate was quickly consumed by their bodies, not an ounce put into energy reserves for the walking that lay ahead; so many miles to go that to think too hard upon the distance would be a death sentence.

The SS pulled their aluminium dishes from within their kit, brushing away invisible germs, giving them a polish with their thumbs in order that they may receive the goodness of the Third Reich. And their dishes were piled high with pea soup and chunks of white bread, chunks of meat and the promise of something with taste, and the steam carried with it the smell of something which would not pass the prisoners' lips for some time to come. So thick was the soup with peas of the SS that it was hard to see the water; what a contrast, the soup of the Jews when compared to that of the guards; there simply was no comparison; there was no relationship between the two. The two soups were as different as were the SS and the Jews.

The snow was also getting much worse, piled high now along the way, falling upon the shaved heads of those that marched along to the beat of the SS curses. The wind was blowing hard and the chill cut into its victims without mercy. But the column pushed on, and then out from the rear came another signal that a SS guard had dealt out his measure of hatred upon one of them, a single shot from a pistol echoing throughout the area, a Jewish woman of forty being kicked from where she lay and into the ditch beyond, her body to fester and decay in the frozen gutter which seemed to follow the road as it disappeared into the distance ahead. But others felt the mercy of the killing, could see how it was an easy way into heaven, to be handed reprieve from the hard walk that lay ahead.

All around them was white with snow, so thick in places that it could devour a man without a trace, but there were no men here, only the Germans of a male persuasion being carried on the backs of carts and the SS with hands on pistols which they used as easily as they used the words, 'your shit', 'you arse', 'you filthy, lazy Jew'.

And the walking continued until they fell upon a train station on the far outskirts of a city unknown.

A SS guard came out from a doorway of the station in front and his voice could be heard congratulating them, the prisoners, in all their glory, showering them with the kindest words they'd heard this day. "You lazy bitches will be taken the remainder of the way by train," said the officer. A few other soldiers could

13

then be seen falling into earshot and orders were passed around, smiles being shared amongst a few, others wearing stern looks as they perused the column of scum, this was followed by the clubbing of the women for they moved too slowly for the likes of Heinrich Himmler, Hitler, and the whole German race.

"Come on, move it," said a soldier of the SS. "We don't have all day," and he struck hard the woman, Ruth, on the back of the head, the little baby of several months in her arms still as dead and frozen as when she'd first picked it up – how did she ever manage to carry the child so far? She fell upon the ground and was hit several times more before the soldier pulled his pistol from his holster. He was the same as most of the other SS, standing there that minute in time in his heavy boots and with a signet ring flashing here and there for everyone to see that he was a real soldier as seen through the eyes of other soldiers, but a monster to those that walked the road under the threats that erupted from within him and the others. They were like worms, grovelling to appease Himmler's and Hitler's every wish; so foul they were that they would be remembered for all time, but for all of the wrong reasons: or should that be 'for all the right reasons', for isn't it right that we remember these savage brutes?

He aimed the weapon and then reconsidered his action: to waste a bullet on one so nearly dead was foolhardy. He locked eyes with another Jew. A snarling grimace then appeared upon the guard's face and he pointed his weapon at the side of the other's head and pulled the trigger. "Look at me like that, you pile of crap." Another prisoner walked on by, past the fallen victim, wiping the blood from her face. "You and you, move that body aside. Quickly now or you'll get the same."

The woman so brutally clubbed to the ground stirred a little and the guard ignored her: let the cold take care of the fallen. As for the prisoner shot in the head: "You should be thankful," said the guard to the others, "for I've just made more room for you on the train," and laughed his heinous laugh.

The SS officer that had given the short speech had managed to push his way through to the point of the commotion, where a few disgruntled voices had been heard to rise, where prisoners were commencing to push from different directions: some towards the empty carriages and others, away.

"What's going on here?" asked the officer.

The soldier stood to attention and reported the incident as was his duty.

"This woman was moving too slowly, sir," said the SS maggot. "It was causing a commotion and so I gave remedy to the situation."

The officer looked down and saw the woman who had been hit several times in the side and back of the head, blood now sporting her skull. He then saw the other, blood already congealed at the wound site where she had been shot.

"No more bullets, private," said the officer. "No more shooting." He raised his voice for all to hear. "Get on board as quickly and quietly as possible or you shall be left to the wilderness, to be delivered your punishment by the hand of the weather. This snow will not stop, so get on board, quickly."

The private could see and feel that this officer was different in some small way. He seemed to care for this sodden lot, just a little, but seemed afraid to announce his feelings to the world in case the Führer should hear of his poor showing.

"Get them on board, private, as quickly as possible. Any problems... drag them to the rear and I'll take care of them personally."

"Yes sir," said the man in SS uniform and commenced with his instructions, kicking the arses of the slow; the old and the frail.

Herded now the women continued to clamber aboard the open carriages at the station, being hit over the back of the head by soldiers too scared to touch them, for they smelt bad and had sores all over their bodies; bruises accompanied with cuts and abrasions. The SS also wished to keep a distance between themselves and the lice which infested some of the women.

The Jews were skinny and all very sick, nothing more than bone in most cases, and where women were once proud owners of breast well shaped and luscious, now lay nothing more than flabby skin against ribcage, perused by others looking through sunken eyes sockets and insane minds, for no one could remain sane in such appalling conditions.

There was silence amongst them as they were forced onto the train, a journey of some five hundred kilometres to be endured. The SS guards were shovelling food into their mouths once more, drinking what water they had and wiping their faces with the rags that they carried as part of their kit, grunting noises coming from them all, like pigs at a trough – but pigs didn't deserve to be affiliated with krauts.

The journey was long and hard, no food or water to be had anywhere. When people died they did so standing up, freezing in place. Bodies of the dead could not be moved until the cramped conditions of the carriages in which they were transported could be vacated; so keep still, and share what warmth can be shared. Not long now, not long until the doors would open for an opportunity to breath and receive fresh water and nourishment, for what lay ahead when the doors did finally open would be Bergen-Belsen, and all knew that Bergen-Belsen was a Shangrila when compared to Auschwitz.

And then the reality of it all hit them hard. Life for them had been a sheer misery, from Auschwitz to Bergen-Belsen, but those of Bergen-Belsen were a dilapidated sight, by far worse off than those currently standing on the train. The prisoners didn't know what to do; stay on the train or get off; which was worse? Never was there a time in history where the unfortunate would cast their eyes upon such a scene as horrific as this 'hell camp' and come to realise that they had had it easy whilst in Auschwitz, but it was only recently that the camp had become as bad as it was and superseded the other camps by becoming the worst in all of known history.

The so-called 'death march' across Germany, train from Dresden, and countless deaths along the way; none of it compared to what was about to unfold. There were twelve tents, seemingly hastily erected, and straw thrown upon the ground to act as a mattress; which would not last long. And so the horrors of being a prisoner, a slave, a dog for which to kick and beat, continues on from one day to the next.

Dishes from which to eat food, if edible food was seen at all, were so few and far between these new inhabitants that to see one was like a vision from heaven. No; tin cans were the way... if they could be secured; and so theft was always present as it was hard to prove ownership of one tin can from another.

These Polish women felt the shame of it all, felt the shame of being a Jew, but why should that be shameful; because it had been instilled within their minds, brainwashed into them every single day of their miserable existence? They looked up and through the barbed wire fence, to see the other Jews of the camp. They, too, were thin and unhealthy, diseased and unsteady upon their feet, but at least they had a barracks which provided better warmth than the thin skin of a useless tent, and a thin layer of straw for a bed.

CHAPTER 2

The camp was in an obvious dilapidated state and it could only get worse before it got any better. The Poles knew very little about the camp itself but it seemed quite obvious, even now, that those at the Russian front were being evacuated to the rear, to this camp, Bergen-Belsen, it taking an influx of disease and wretchedness from the others camps right across Germany, from all quarters in the face of the Third Reich, in this, its downfall.

From high upon its post flew the flag of Germany, a true sign of cruelty within the world, and nothing could be more cruel than this sign, nothing more cruel was there in the entire world than the one that was proudly displayed by the Nazis and their regime.

Row upon row of wooden buildings covered the ground, hastily built refuges where the unfortunate were forced to live out their lives as prisoners. The wooden huts were where the weak stayed and died, where the able bodied were cast upon hard labour, and guards inflicted what they called justice as they saw fit.

Some of the huts had no bunks to speak of and comprised little less than a floor covered in bodies, some dead, but all diseased in some way. The dead would be removed in the morning; always in the morning. Blankets were strewn all over, were hard to come by, but a godsend. To lice it was like heaven, and to disease a haven for spreading its malignity as best it could, going unchecked and free to cast its evil spell upon everyone within the wire cordon known as Bergen-Belsen.

And more and more people arrived each day. Where did they all come from? As already stated, from all over Europe it would seem, those closest to the front line being evacuated to Bergen-Belsen. It was too impossible to believe, but worse was to come. It was hard to believe that there were around 10,000 people sharing a single toilet.

CHAPTER 3

Everyone was woken at 4:45am and the gears for the day's work were shifted ever so slowly into neutral and then engaged.

Different parts of the camp were treated differently and standards of work and living varied from one to the other, but in general terms it was all the same to most of them: so little sleep, and so little food; life in general was such a misery. Hungarian Jews had it the best; being any other nationality of 'exchange' Jew was also fortunate – someone would have to one day have it explained what it meant to be 'fortunate'. No one had the energy to continue as they did, but not to do so would reap the truncheon blow of a guard, or even worse; a bullet to the head - but was a bullet to the head so awful?

It was 6:00am and all prisoners, from all sectors of the camp, were called to assembly in the open, many parades assembled around the camp; which occurred regardless of weather conditions, rain, sleet or snow. The worst thing of all wasn't as simple as the weather though, but the sheer stupidity of the SS and their inability to count. If the roll call was accurate and the numbers added up then the prisoners could continue on to work; in the fields, the kitchen, or elsewhere where shelter might be attained; even if only limited. It was a matter of being damned no matter what the result. If they go to work, they might be warmed, but the sheer agony of sitting upon a stall for eleven hours or more in a single day could be torture upon the back. And what of those poor bastards, the men, who had to surrender themselves to hard labour attached to the 'tree commando', where even the very stumps of the trees had to be dug from the ground in order to be fed to the furnaces within the kitchens. They cut and saw all day, every day; fir and pine; hail, rain or sunshine. The wood was needed in order to prepare the food for the entire camp, but what did they get but a bowl of watery soup; it was sheer stupidity. But to stand for hours on end at roll call when inclement weather was inbound was a recipe for disaster, prisoners literally falling to the ground dead. It was here that prisoners were ordered to carry the dead aside to be cremated later. One might pity the poor mother of a teenager when she saw her child fall upon the ground, her soul giving up the fight to survive, but another would think of the extra ration that might be available to eat at the end of the day. It was all a matter of survival, and the strongest had a better chance than most.

The body of the deceased would be carried away by the prisoners at the convenience of the master doing the count, carried to the crematorium for burning. The crematorium was a lonely station, big enough to burn one body at a time. Two boys were stationed here, two Jews whose sole task it was to cremate the dead. The furnace was kept alive, all day; the bodies kept coming, all day; the work was endured, all day. This was their life; this was what they endured. They talk to no one. The crematorium was a small building built of red brick and surrounded by a seven-foot fence. This was the loneliest station of the camp.

Work was from 6:30am to 11:30am and if the prisoners were lucky – ah; such a silly choice of words, but such words are the only ones available to represent the good fortune called food – then they were marched back to parade outside the huts for another roll call and lunch. The watery soup that the men had worked so hard to help provide, by digging away at roots, was now fed them all, but the hunger still existed, hadn't even waivered the slightest. What had gone down their throats seemed like nothing at all, but not having this ridiculous portion of nourishment would soon see the death of them all through the pain of starvation.

There was plenty of work to be had which was hard on the back, though allowed for much conversation. The work was in the large horse stable which was made of stone, and provided were the tools of the prisoner's trade: tables, hard stools, and plenty of shoes. They mustered around as though they were bees to a honey pot, drawn by the scent of their conviction, to seek a little freedom from that which encased them all. But the freedom was hard fought, even for the hours of the day in which they toiled over the pile of shoes, thousands upon thousands of second hand shoes that were piled high in front of them all.

This was the Shoe Commando where mostly the young girls worked, fourteen year-olds that were looked over as though meat in a market: the SS always had a keen eye for what might bring them pleasure at a later date, but as the months rolled on, and the task became too much for the women, men were employed, a total of six hundred souls conducting what was rather meaningless slave labour with the pain searing up and down their legs and backs.

Quite often, in the hustle and bustle of roll call, it was the accidental allocation of an older woman to the task which was an oversight for the SS guard but a relief – in most cases – for the woman of age and maturity. But the older, more intelligent, were harder to be swayed by the SS guards, and those that were married were seldom seen flirting with the enemy... although there were some that did the unthinkable by sleeping with a guard, or the blockführer, in order to bring an extra ration of bread and turnip to their husband's table, to provide additional nutrition where it was needed the most, for the work amongst the trees was very hard indeed.

After being appointed to the 'shoe commando' by the blockführer, it was time to go and acquaint themselves with the shoes and put up with the unpleasantness of undesired conversation, where roasts, steaks, sandwiches, cakes and food of all description was spoken of, and did nothing to help them through the days of hunger that were pressed upon them all. The labour was quite intensive and it was ordered that each woman was to rip apart 40 pairs of dusty shoes in a single day, where the leather was to be split into three piles upon the tables, each being allocated as either 'good leather', 'cloth', or 'waste'.

It was a form of retribution... no; it was outright justified that when the prisoners saw that a guard had turned his attention away from the table, literally turned his ugly head in another direction, that they did damage to a good piece of leather hence removing it from the service of the Führer, a commodity that could otherwise service his crumbling war machine, for the good of no purpose than to satisfy his desires of demented disposition in ruling the world.

The cloth was something the inmates took care to ensure went to good use and was gathered as something more pleasant on which to wipe their arses when sitting on a toilet, or over a cold iron bar of one of the makeshift toilets, sucking in the disgusting fumes of faeces from the pit below where they sat or crouched, holding their guts in their palms for pain was often present when relieving the bowels. With this said it was not surprising to note that the SS guards did not attend to their flock as well as they should and the number of pairs of shoes attended to by each prisoner was usually well below the required number, some seeing to it that they did as few as fifteen pairs in a single week when more than two hundred pairs was due – due for whom; that damned crazy bastard, Hitler?

Work for no pay! Work as slaves! The damn Nazis were such lowly scum that the prisoners would prefer to step in dog shit wearing expensive shoes... damn shoes; the thought of shoes; more, and more, and more damn shoes. Shoes during the day, shoes in their nightmares, but not many pairs of shoes on very many feet... so few could walk around with the knowledge that what they stepped on would not quiche between their toes.

Work for the women was scarce but in particular the kitchen duty was sought, especially towards the latter part of their unjustified sentences just prior to their rescue by the allies. Although they dared ro be caught, it was sheer bliss to cram as much peel into one's mouth as possible, or to hide something of a potato in the boots... those poor men; their work could be devastating. Easy was the work with the shoes but hell was the felling of trees, digging of roots, carting of wood, and the stirring of the huge kettles in which water was boiled within the kitchens; it simply sapped the energy from within when energy wasn't to spare; it was sheer torment to work when not an ounce of energy was available to even talk, cough or sneeze.

The mess kettles were huge and varied in size from around

twenty to fifty litres, a mammoth task in itself to portage when full, let alone empty. Those whose duty it was to carry the kettles empty had the task cut out for them, but to pull off the same miracle when full of watery soup was sheer agony.

Then back to work, from 12:30pm to 6:30pm, another roll call and then back to the barracks to be drowned in a combined misery and soiled existence; one shared by all.

One old woman had fallen whilst being beaten on parade. She stayed there upon the ground in the mud. No one helped her, for to do so would mean death or bunker, and bunker usually meant death, so you couldn't win. She died where she lay, to be carted away in the morning.

As for now; now they spend time together, male and female, where husbands and wives could provide those encouraging words that there was light beyond the tunnel entrance. A wife would present a slice of bread for the husband and he would shake his head, saying 'No, I've managed to have something before returning to the hut'. So the wife eats some of the bread on insisting that they share it. The husband feels awkward that he should take from his wife but the wife knows that the husband didn't really have any brea earlier on, that he was simply offering all for her to eat. And throughout the barracks, wives and husbands tried their hardest to pull the blanket over the eyes of the other, lying as best they could in order for their companion in life to have something more than watery soup served from large kettles along with a portion of stinking bread.

And so each fights to find a different way in which to provide the other with that added nourishment, but each, in their own way, knew that the other was tricking them into eating what sits before them. The wife would give everything for the husband and the husband for the wife. The hard labour of the men saw to it that they needed twice as much more to eat than the women, where working long hours in the 'tree commando' and fields saps them of all energy, making them more skinny and susceptible to disease as each day passes them by.

At 7:45pm the men and women would separate into their own

quarters. They had special treatment and the empowering of a partnership between a man and woman provides them with greater incentive and opportunity for survival. But now the work was done and they no longer had to wait their turn to go to the latrines, but stagger off as they pleased, to be inundated by the fail stench of human shame orchestrated by the blocked pipes, and the SS guards watched over the camp to ensure that all remained peaceful and that no one tried to escape.

CHAPTER 4

A severe storm hit the camp and several tents were ripped apart. The Polish women stood in the pouring rain and cold wind. It was a shocking surprise when half a dozen guards turned up out of the darkness, to press upon them their commands.

"You, Jews," shouted one of the guards, a tall man that seemed to overshadow the other by his side. "Move; quickly, I don't have all day. This rain is pouring down my neck as you fart around. Leave your possessions; move it!"

Judith looked around at the bustling crowd and saw that everyone was moving in a panic. The hail fell upon them, small stones of ice which bounced off of their bald heads.

"Come on, slut; I haven't all day," came the command of a guard as he lashed out with his truncheon, knocking a woman to the ground. Many others continued on, stepping over her, pushing her into the mud. "Move it!"

A bolt of lightning then struck somewhere outside the wire and for a brief moment the lights of the guards' towers flickered off and then on again.

"Leave everything, hurry up."

Judith heard the words but couldn't believe them. She had no possessions, knew of very few that had. Tin cans were all and if clothing was possessed then they would have been worn, no protection from the cold of the night when sleeping in a tent.

"Oh, Judith... help me," came a lonesome voice and Judith looked around as she was shoved alone.

"Hurry up," and a guard kicked her in the arse: better a foot than a bullet.

Judith thought she'd recognised the voice of the woman. It was an elderly lady she'd met just the other day, one that had shared with her a half-slice of bread as she was too sick to even eat.

"Help me, Judith."

Judith looked upon the face of the fallen woman and tried to fight the crowd, but the crowd was too strong; and just then a guard came up behind the woman on the ground and stepped upon her head, driving it into the mud. The sadistic look upon his face was etched, forever more, upon Judith's mind.

There was nothing that Judith could do but give praise that she, herself, was alive.

They were quickly shuffled off to the shed, the horse stable, where shoes were normally being ripped apart, but it was swamped with almost a foot of water and so the misery of their existence continued.

"In here, quickly," yelled a guard. "Find yourselves somewhere dry and out of the rain."

Was he serious, or simply stupid beyond all contemplation?

It was amazing that the guards had acted so quickly by providing shelter but then they turned their cheeks and started to laugh when the leaking roof deposited more water onto the deepening pool that currently splashes against the prisoners' ankles.

It was a joke beyond all jokes, moving from a station in the open, to another which was full of water and leaked like a sieve.

"Be quiet, all of you," shouted another guard as the six of them gathered around briefly to discuss the situation.

"Let's leave them to their misery," said one. "It's damn cold and I'm wet through. Why should we suffer for these... scum of the earth they are?"

"You follow orders, just like me," came the answer. "Come on; let's get out of here."

A pair of eyes was then cast upon the prisoners. "You will stay here until you're moved," ordered a guard. "If you leave this stable without the authority of the SS, you will be taken to the bunker."

Judith stood as did the others, nowhere to sit but in the water that surrounded them like a lake. There they stayed for the duration of the night until they were removed the next day, removed to another part of the camp in order for the shoe commando to recommence with its work upon the shoes.

CHAPTER 5

It's during times of stormy weather that the greatest of entertainment could be attained, although it was true to say that such entertainment could be had at almost any time.

The dark loneliness of the night, where rain, wind or hail might shield the happenings in a particular washroom, a corporal sat upon a stall and had a grin upon his face a mile wide. It's a dirty grin, one filled with the dirt of a sadistic mind, perpetrating to commit, always to commit, some act of attrition against the weak.

Corporal 'Red' Mueller would love to watch two girls taking a bath together, but then again, he would love to watch more than this. It was proposed, once, that he liked to seek the attention of boys, but so young the children would be that it was hard to tell the difference between male and female, where his advances, although less warranted, were just as enjoyable to him: but even children craved food.

It was to his great joy and entertainment that what followed a romp in the shower, by the light of a small globe or even a lantern at times that the power might be out, would satisfy his sexual desires to the very depths of his fantasies. He knew what he wanted, and he too often received it.

His mind was corrupted by years of hatred for the Jews, and years of condemning them as he felt they deserved to be condemned. What was it for him to care what they felt; they were nothing more than pests? Society didn't want them and if society didn't want them then they were turned over to the likes of him, in camps which robbed people of their right to live in freedom. It was nothing to him at all and as he sipped on the small glass of sherry he'd watch with full delight as two girls washed each other down with soapy water.

The girls would be looked after, of course, adequately fed and watered, just like cattle, for they were favourites now and forever. They were pleasing to him and acted out the play that harassed his mind. All day long he would be thinking of these nights of luxury: damned if he cared what others thought, and so as he quickly glanced around to ensure all was quiet and that he was alone as the play to his front continued to unfold.

It might be lights on at 5:00am and lights out at 9:00pm, but when you had rank and position the entertainment of the night could keep you as warm as a good glass of spirit. His sherry he could go without, but go without his luxuries such as this and he was just another man in the system that thought of different ways to ridicule, beat, and hamper.

It was a courtesy of the Third Reich that was little known elsewhere in the world where blockführers felt it their prime duty to watch the women undress and shower, be they alone, in twos and threes, or en masse.

Mueller would continue to satisfy himself as he watched and after he could take it no more he would have his way with both of them, and at the end of his excitement he would reward both with extra slices of bread, and maybe something more appetising, a slice of cheese or a sliver of fatty bacon.

Oh, how grand it was to be Mueller, so grand that he loved to hear his name called out from within a crowd of women. He could only congratulate himself on his good work and good fortune. He loved himself like he loved no other. He would do all he could to ensure he didn't jeopardise his position.

CHAPTER 6

Being sent to work was either good or bad, and sometimes both. It consisted of the evil doings of the SS more than anything else; but food was all important.

It seemed ludicrous and a sheer waste of time to be standing there on parade for well over an hour in order for the guards to do their count, to add the numbers together, to see how they stacked up in semblance to what should be the correct number; but it was carried out several times in a single day, if not more.

The total number of dead, for the time being, was being recorded, as too, were the numbers reporting sick each day, along with those being given the permission from the medical officer to take the day off, and to have 'so-and-so' many days of rest.

The numbers were tallied and the barracks checked. It appeared that the doctor had awarded several with bed rest, which only came when a temperature of over 39 degrees Celsius was registered on his – no doubt – faulty equipment, for the doctor cared as little for the Jews as did the SS guards.

"You are lucky today," said a guard who was familiar with one of the women on the bunk. "There is much work to be done." He looked around the barrack hut and turned one last time to the woman lying there with horrible pain searing through her. "No soup for you today. Only those that work will be given good food."

She wondered where the 'good' food came from, because she never saw any of it.

"I'll let the other women know when they return. If I see anyone feeding you then you'll be shot, thrown in the bunker, and then shot again. You stupid Jews; you're so lazy that it makes me puke."

He continued outside and reported to the sergeant that his numbers on the sick, as earlier reported, were correct, and so the adding up of numbers continued.

Shortly after this exercise of stupidity came the call for a small group to make its way to the 'peel kitchen' where many hours of labour was to be suffered by the hand of their puppet masters. They, a small group of the poor souls that made up the prisoner formation, were segregated from the others and formed up shortly after roll call to ensure that they were ready for the work that was to be allocated to them all, to be shuffled away under the heavy threat of beatings to a kitchen in readiness to peel... ah, turnips.

They reached the building in which they were to work and all were quick to enter, for it was best to be seated in one area as opposed to another, enabling more turnip peel to be eaten; whether or not it was digested was another matter, for diarrhoea and throwing up were complaints often heard about.

It was here in the kitchen that what could have been classified as 'young and strapping lads' simply stood around in their clean uniform of the SS and watched the prisoners, with nothing better to do, it would seem, than to cuss and curse.

"Can you believe this, Judith?" came the question in a whisper, Sonja careful not to be the victim of a guard's malice.

"What is that?" asked Judith, sadly, continuing along with her work as did the others. She wasn't feeling well today for the 'death march' had taken much out of her, in spirit and emotionally.

"That it takes so many young SS guards to watch over a heap of turnips."

"I heard that the turnips, too, are scared," said Franzi.

"Shut your stinking mouths!" yelled a guard from the rear. "If I hear another word I'll come over there and shit on your head and put the rest of you against the fence."

Here they sat within the confines of a small room, upon benches of rotting wood which sat upon tin drums, canisters which were at one time full to the brim with nourishment but now served other purposes, at a time when the war had confiscated much material and from many quarters.

It was the season for turnips: it always seemed to be the season for turnips, in particular at Bergen-Belsen. Turnips was the staple, a commodity suffered day in and day out, breakfast and dinner, sometimes in the form of a soup comprising little more than a splash of vegetable matter amongst a portion of ladled water. But these turnips before them were practically rotten, full of larvae and too foul to be eaten by a human, let alone a pig. And then it came, the answer for them all.

"You swine will work until the bags are empty," said the corporal in charge, Otto Calesson. "And if a single piece should pass your lips then you'll feel the wrath of the SS as never felt before. Now peel."

The sacks delivered to them were huge and the smell of dust filled the air as each was opened to reveal its contents, and with a blunt knife the women went to work peeling the vegetables in preparation for them to be eaten in one way or another.

Franzi picked up a turnip and her thumb fell into it. It was rotten right through to the core. She wanted to see it thrown out but knew better than that. To be seen throwing food away would result in severe punishment. She took her knife and did what she could, careful not to damage it further, but by the time she'd finished with her task the turnip flesh was all over her hand.

A truncheon blow was quickly felt upon the back of her head from which she winced.

"Take care, shit-bag," said the punishing guard, Karl. "Now clean your fingers."

Franzi fidget to get up when another blow was felt upon the back of her head, a little harder than the first. She'd do well not to provoke him further.

"No, you stay there. Lick your hands clean; come on," ordered Karl. "I want to see them cleaned."

Another guard close by, laughed out loud.

"Come on, hurry up; I'm serious," said Karl as Franzi began to lick her fingers clean.

"No, not like that, you stupid whore. Flick your tongue out, like you mean it. Come on; pretend you're a snake."

The other guard laughed again.

And Franzi entertained the guard until her fingers were clean and the guard had had enough. He moved on and she took another turnip from the pile.

The shame of the exercise didn't stop there, however, for there was some good peel that was going to waste, pushed aside and out of reach, pushed from prying eyes, hungry mouths, and stomachs that grumbled away with expectation that never came.

There seemed to be so much peel that it was impossible.

One of the women, so overcome by hunger, could help herself no longer; it was Judith. The sheer agony of seeing a piece of peel hanging from the blade of her knife was too much to bear. There were several guards present but seemed to be talking amongst themselves at the moment, and so many women in the kitchen that the situation merited the offering which sat before her upon the edge of the knife.

Sonja saw the look in Judith's eyes and warned her not to try the impossible, a whisper so low that it was hardly heard, a warning through partially open lips.

Judith looked out of the corner of her eye to Sonja and then quickly flashed the peel into her mouth, swallowing it whole, the soreness of her throat almost bringing her to convulsion, and then came the stabbing in the arm as a guard from behind her lashed at her with a bayonet positioned upon his rifle, the blade of his instrument of death penetrating her flesh and quickly bringing blood to the surface of her worn rags, infection to come about if given the chance, but from the mouth of the guard came insults and slander, a clear indication that she would soon see death.

"You filthy whore-thief!" yelled Karl. "What manner of prisoner are you to take that which is not permitted?"

She didn't cry or scream out when stabbed but simply put her hand where the wound was, and the guards gathered around to commence their mockery.

"You're a thief," said Otto. "Nothing more than a common thief, you Jewish whore."

Karl spat down upon her as she looked up into his eyes, a thick dollop of spit ending up on her face. She wiped it away with her hand, blood replacing the wet, a clean spot then emerging from beneath the hours of airborne dirt and labour.

"She's washing herself," said the same guard that had laughed before and now laughed out loud once again.

"The slut likes to be clean," said the third. "They say a whore will groom herself before a night with many men."

"How many guards did you sleep with in Auschwitz, slut?" asked Otto.

The other soldiers found the insubordinate nature of the piece of filth before them nothing more than a simple insult to their position as held by the SS; she was blatantly disobeying the order to give an answer.

"Take her, I'll be along shortly," said Otto and two guards picked the woman up, one either side, and commenced to drag her away in silence. "Make her walk," said Otto. "Use your bayonet."

The private, Hans, nodded and felt a little out of place, accepting orders for what should have been common sense, and in front of a group of hapless Jews. He was new to the establishment and needed to be seen as a good man amongst his peers, not to be seen as useless or intimidated. Without warning he lifted his arm across his body and lashed out with his elbow.

Judith fell to the floor almost unconscious, blood spurting from her nose and her mouth, several teeth having been knocked out of place, loosened over the weeks of travelling from the gas chambers of Auschwitz to this place in the middle of the forest, this camp of hell that was sitting on cleared ground in the middle of nowhere, little semblance of humanity anywhere to be seen, human life seen for what it was: very, very sad.

"Get up, you lazy bitch," ordered the young SS soldier, Hans, the new boy on the block. "Get up before I strangle your scrawny neck." He grabbed at a small tuft of hair that she had upon her head and as he pulled her to her feet the hair fell out into his hand. He brushed it away in disgust against his trouser leg.

Otto laughed. "Be careful, Hans. This piece of crap might not have lice, but she might have something else to pass onto you, some deadly disease that can't be cured."

The fidgeting young private showed his unsettled feelings and he pushed the woman along. He'd heard of the diseases carried by these lowlife scum and couldn't shake it from his mind. He was young and immature and would no doubt receive a visit in the night from some of the men, to remind him of his training and to deliver a speech on how to treat the prisoners like the dogs they were, and even though he did give the prisoner, Judith, a good hiding with his elbow, it simply wasn't enough.

CHAPTER 7

Judith felt alone now, even if escorted by two guards, and she was forced into a small room of which she had little knowledge.

"Get in there," said Hans as he pushed from behind with an open palm.

Judith fell forward and hit her head against the floor before she stood once more, half dazed from the hit to the head.

"Corporal Otto will be along shortly," said Hans, "and he will not be kind. You should have heeded the warnings you were given, but now; you will receive punishment."

Hans turned himself outside as did the other with him.

"What will Otto do?" asked Hans.

"Something special," said Karl. "It's always something special with Otto. You're in for a real treat. I know exactly the type of man he is."

"Tell me," urged Hans.

"No, you can wait," said Karl. "You will see soon enough with your own eyes, and when you do you'll be happy that you waited for an answer. It is always better to see rather than hear. Remember that, Hans, always remember. There is nothing like true experience."

"Have you experienced much? Have you been here long?" asked Hans.

"I have been here for more than a year and have seen things grow worse by the month, now they grow worse by the day, but I don't care. I hate the stink in this camp, all thanks to those stupid, shit-eating, Jews. They should have all remained in Auschwitz."

"Is it true then, what they say about Auschwitz?" asked Hans.

"I believe so. I have spoken with some that have come from there. They gas them by the thousands," said Karl as he looked into Hans' eyes, seeing a little disbelief and a little horror. "Imagine that, ah, Hans; thousands of them killed, just like that. That's one way to get rid of them I suppose. It's got to be better than looking after the swine."

Nigel B.J. Clayton

"I knew a Jew," said Hans, "a long time again... we weren't friends but... he was of good position and had plenty of money."

"Those scum," snarled Karl as he kicked at the closed door of the bunker. "They steal turnip peels like they stole jobs from us before the war. They don't deserve to live, not a stinking one of them."

A dog bark was then heard and Hans turned with Karl to see Otto coming down the passageway with Juana Bormann beside him, a wolfhound at her heels. She was one of the most hated SS guards in the establishment.

"Otto has brought Juana and her pet. Now you will see," said Karl.

Juana Bormann was a vicious looking sort, her face screwed up like a bull terrier snarling. She was known throughout as 'the woman with the dogs' and was renowned for setting her wolfhounds upon the prisoners, to tear them apart, to rip them to pieces, but she wasn't fond of seeing the dogs put to any danger: only the weak were mauled by her dogs. This wretched woman had no feelings, less than a man of the SS in fact. If she was put into a cage with a male SS guard, and each was to fight to the death, the bets would be even.

CHAPTER 8

Judith was locked in the cell by herself. She looked around as the two guards shut the cell door.

It looked like an interrogation room except there was no office furniture and had but a few small cracks in the masonry of the walls. The floor was made of stone, cold and uninviting, covered in stains, and from an adjoining room she could hear the mumbles of a female having been tormented half to death, seemingly half crazed beyond belief. This was the bunker and had but a solitary item of worth in it, that being a hard wooden bed.

This entire prison was a cesspool and with the thought came the feelings of a cramp within her gut, and she was forced onto all fours. What soup she had received the night before, and this morning before being called upon to work, now spilled from her bowels and ran over her thigh before she could manage to stand properly. She had no energy at all, hardly enough to peel those sodden turnips, let alone to have enough energy within her to stand quickly.

The smell of the shit hit her nostrils almost immediately, the rankness of it slapping her in the face, but it was less than what an outsider would suffer for she was used to the foul stench of the barracks already, used to the treatment suffered at the hands of these German bastards. The Germans; whipping was too good for them, so too was a bullet in the head. She only wished that one day they would get the justice that they all deserved.

She felt so poorly, so bad, so meaninglessly, depressed and scared. She was alone, had blood caked over her face and shit all down the inside of her leg as well as out. She longed for life but also wished for death. She couldn't have both. What she really wanted was for something she could not have: freedom.

She didn't wish to sit just yet, for the bed might actually be clean. The last thing she wished to do was soil it, but she felt so tired.

She could hear the men talking outside and was rather

concerned by the path the conversation took and then she could hear a dog bark.

She had no idea of knowing what was install for her for she was relatively new to Bergen-Belsen, but she hoped to learn quickly of this place in order to outwit the system and to survive to see the day when freedom was dealt all that waited within the huts and the kitchens, and the forest; all of those in the 'shoe commando', the 'tree commando', and every other work party that had been invented by the SS; all should be allowed to go free, every person here in this camp except the stinking SS guards. It was her dream.

Further talking then took place outside the door of her cell and it opened to reveal the two guards, the corporal, and one she'd not seen before, a woman with a dog.

The dog appeared well behaved for the moment, for it was awaiting a command from the woman.

"Karl," said Otto. "You help our new friend here, Hans, to experience what it is to issue true punishment. And don't forget to leave something for the dog."

Judith was horrified by the words which she understood. She seldom spoke in German, but she understood enough to get her through her days.

Hans didn't let the corporal down, he went in beside Karl and together they beat Judith from head to toe, beating her with their truncheons, upon the arms, legs and head. They kept beating her until she was almost dead, laying on the ground in pools of her own diarrhoea. She was so badly beaten that all she could do was lay there in a heap and hope for the best, but also wishing that she was dead.

"Okay Hans, that's enough," ordered Otto. "Juana; if you please."

"Thank you, Corporal," said the dog-faced woman. She then antagonized the dog, pulled on his chain and got him angered. The dog's teeth showed in all their glory as the lips around them curled away with its show of strength. A few orders were then given to the dog, short, clear and concise orders which were issued as the dog's leash was unclipped. The dog fell upon its victim and ripped poor Judith apart, sinking its teeth into her and ripped flesh from flesh. Her face was the first thing the dog went for, sinking its teeth into her nose, mouth and cheeks, and within just a few short seconds the face became so disfigured that it could not be recognised as human.

Judith was simply another victim of the guards' cruelty.

CHAPTER 9

The duties performed by the two boys at the crematorium were ceaseless. No sooner did they seem to be on top of the situation and then more bodies arrived for them to incinerate.

The boys had not mingled with others of the camp for a very long time. They were locked in at their post and would do their job as ordered by the authority. They were fed better than most, for the work was usually quite hard and always lonely.

Samuel and Maurice had been together for so long now that they felt as though they were brothers, maybe not of kin, but true brothers all the same. They thought alike, ate the same, and shared the same miserable task. They knew each other inside out and conversation between them was sometimes scarce because they knew everything there was to know about one another.

A body was delivered and they loaded it into the oven, placed the wood beneath the oven and then torched it. It was easy, so easy that a trained monkey could do the task with its eyes sewn shut.

A guard approached the crematorium and the two boys looked up. It wasn't meal time and there was nobody in sight, so what was it that this bastard of a guard wanted?

"Shit-lips," yelled the guard, Oskar. "And you, Arse-face."

The boy's knew their names. They were christened some time ago now. The guards' humour was sometimes deplorable to say the least.

"There's to be no burning today," ordered Oskar.

The boys knew that an order couldn't be ignored, but the boys were safe. They were at their post, following the orders of the camp commandant.

"Yes, but these bodies," pointed out Samuel.

"You shut your mouth, or I'll have you both whipped," said Oskar. "You do as you're told," and although an explanation was never required the guard felt that it was a small price to pay, and so gave one. "The wind is blowing very strongly today and the smell will fall towards the Panzer barracks. We have had complaints before. Now do as you are told or I'll see to it that your rations are halved."

The guard turned around and departed the vicinity of the boys' responsibility.

"What are we to do with these ten bodies?" asked Maurice. "Isn't it enough that we have to burn these poor bastards, and now we have to spend the whole day and night looking at them?"

"The wind might change direction later," said Samuel.

"The guard won't return, and even if he does it won't be till late, and I don't want to have to burn bodies all night long. I don't think I can take it much more."

"You don't talk like that, Maurice. We do the job we have to do. It's a way to stay alive. There are many dying from starvation... we are lucky."

"I don't think it's lucky," said Maurice. "This is torture. Every day I spend in this shithole I keep thinking about seeing my mother turn up. What am I to do if my mother turns up dead and I have to burn her? What if she's naked and I have to shove her into the furnace like common garbage?"

"I will do the work," answered Samuel, supportively. "I will see to it that she is given a proper send off, not a quick shove into the fire. Trust me, Maurice. I will handle it if the time arrives, but I feel confident that she'll live."

"So what shall we do now?" asked Maurice.

"We'll prepare the furnace and load a body in place. If we hear nothing by morning then we'll start work again."

"I hate this stinking job. I feel dirty eating food which is payment for doing this... unkind thing. There's no sermon, not of any description. We shove and light and burn. That is all we do, all day long, and sometimes into the night when there is not enough time by day."

"It will be okay, Maurice," insisted Samuel. "We'll rest as much as we can today and hopefully clear this lot away later."

Maurice smiled and went to get into his cot and Samuel did the same. They would continue with their work later.

CHAPTER 10

By late afternoon the wind had changed direction but the guard didn't turn up. The burning would have to wait until morning if orders weren't received along with the main meal of the day.

Samuel awoke first and got to his feet. He helped himself to some water and then looked over to his friend.

There was a sudden felt shock and insurmountable fear penetrated every single pore of his body, for Maurice had masterfully hung himself from the ceiling of the crematorium, having used a piece of rope that was his belt.

Maurice had killed himself and without warning.

Samuel immediately flung himself to his friend, to lift him up and relieve the strain of the rope against his neck, but it was no good for Maurice was stone cold; lifeless.

Samuel let go of the body and let it dangle as he cried for his friend that hung there. A little wind was blowing into the furnace room and so the body swayed a little from side to side.

What was the meaning of it all? Why was death so prevalent in this horrible place? Day after day he and Maurice had cremated bodies and now Maurice was dead. Samuel didn't know what to think, what to do, how to feel. His only friend in the world was gone.

Samuel decided right then and there that Maurice would be cremated, but he would serve a ceremony that his friend so deserved. Maurice was concerned for his mother, concerned for the others that came this way, concerned that little favour was done to anyone that died for there wasn't any service to speak of.

Samuel knew that he wasn't well endowed with the ability to give proper sermon but he did all that he could for his friend, and although he didn't yet have clearance to commence with lighting the furnace he went ahead and did so anyway. If a guard came running down to sling insults or threats then Samuel would tell the guard where he could shove his orders.

And so a brief ceremony was undertaken and Maurice was

given the send-off that he so deserved... as all men and women deserved; and as expected a guard was seen walking briskly down the road and even from such a distance Samuel could hear the abuse quite clearly.

It was for him alone, Samuel, to decide his own fate, but to live without the companionship of his friend would simply not do.

Committing Maurice to the flames, therefore, was the last duty that Samuel performed and as he looked over towards the guard he knew immediately what he had to do, for he could take it no more. He would not surrender himself to the whims of the men that held him in captivity like a caged animal.

Samuel was mad to the bone, mad beyond all contemplation from the job he had done these past seven months or more; he was mad with the task he had been provided with. He was no different than his friend, Maurice. He no longer had a clear picture of what it meant to be human and so he stuffed his mouth with twigs, shoving them deep down his throat until he suffocated, until he died by his own hands.

And the month of December was not good for the camp commandant, Josef Kramer, it being the same for the month before when Kramer was not yet posted, where there were between one and two hundred deaths a month: and the number was growing at an alarming rate.

For Kramer there was no choice, the burning of the dead would continue and so two new men were appointed to the task, two new men with fresh minds and the ability to perform their duty well. The fire would be kept burning; the burning of the corpses must continue.

CHAPTER 11

On the 22nd of December, Kramer had instigated a new system where men were promoted to what would become known as 'kapo'; but now it was January and as he saw his plans being hatched, and his orders put into place, he rubbed his hands together in glee. He did this due to the overcrowding of the camp and the ease by which control could be maintained. It was far easier for a SS guard to look after a half dozen, lowlife scum called kapo, than it was to look after thousands of hapless Jews. The thought disgusted him, gave him pains in the stomach. He hated the Jews, despised them like nothing he despised before.

Kapos would be willing to go amongst the death and decay, weeding out the lazy from the sick, organising the prisoners for work parties which needed to be filled by those deserving such horrendous positions, such as the duties performed by the 'tree commando'.

A kapo would have little choice but to see to it that work was performed and that the prisoners were maintained control of. The last thing a kapo needed was to be cuffed behind the ear by a SS guard or thrown amongst the prisoners of whom he had treated so poorly. It was a win-win situation for the guards and the kapos were their puppets, there to have their strings pulled.

For such duties and position a blind eye was often turned so that the dreaded kapo could have his way with the prisoners as he saw fit, taking from them what he wanted, be it their jewellery for a slice of bread, or the virginity of a young girl for a small chunk of cheese.

Yes indeed, Kapo, such a dirty word, and in a majority of the cases, too, a position of rank which was a reward to those of filthy and dilapidated mind, where want for sexual pleasure and handing out severe beatings went hand in hand. You couldn't have one without the other. To be promoted a kapo, or to be an assistant to a kapo, was so unexpectedly received and received well, for only those prisoners of political or criminal prestige would be granted such a position of favour within the camp, and with favour came many kickbacks.

A kapo was a prisoner in charge of prisoners, and many were more vicious than the average SS guard that roamed the grounds with whip in one hand and pistol in the other.

Kasimir Cegielski was but one such depraved kapo who had rotting teeth in his mouth and he stunk horribly, but he was a man nevertheless and able to get things done. He was a good manipulator and sucked up well to the guards in uniform and played them for the poor eyesight they sometimes suffered when watching over the barracks.

Kasimir saw an opportunity one day that simply couldn't be passed up, for the woman involved looked so beautiful. If he could only get some food into her then she might go unspoiled and last him well, to serve him as he so desired.

He was in the barracks which was being cleared for roll call when he noticed her reaching down for something on the floor. He quickly stepped over to her side and leaned down, touching her on the arm rather gently, squeezing it with great affection before she pulled away and looked in the other direction, to move over to where a shawl hung upon a nail near a crud-filled window.

"Hello," said Kasimir. "Do you know who I am?"

"Yes, I do," said the young woman. She was rather fit and healthy when she'd first arrived, but now the wear and tear of camp life was commencing to take its toll upon her. He must save her. She didn't feel herself, in this horrible place, and felt the hollowness within her grow by the day, a great void that seemed to swallow her whole.

"What's your name?"

"It's Henny."

"Well, Henny," started Kasimir, "is there anything I can do for you?"

"No; no, I don't think so," and she pulled the shawl down and placed it around her shoulders, happy to have something warm to throw around her during the cold winter months.

"Are you warm?"

"Yes, thank you," said Henny and then tried to push past him. "I must be on parade for roll call, or punishment will be expected," and the last of the occupants of the barracks exit to leave them alone.

"Oh, no; that's quite alright, Henny,' said Kasimir as he put his hand into a small pouch he carried and pulled out a hunk of cheese.

Henny's eyes lit up as though seeing the wonder of fire for the very first time, a flame flickering in the breeze. She could even smell the cheese for what it was... a life saver.

"Would you like a taste?"

"It looks so... I'm starving," said Henny. "And so is my husband, but I can't pay you much. Here, take my shawl."

"I don't want to deprive you of your shawl," said Kasimir with a faint smile, ignoring the fact that she had a husband; in fact it helped his cause, greatly. "Can't we just be friends?"

"Friends?"

"Yes, that's all."

Henny looked at the cheese. It was a large piece in her eyes, the largest she'd seen in a long time, big enough for her and her husband. They hadn't been married long and he had been taken away to work in the 'tree commando'.

The 'tree commando', work designed for strong young men, where cutting down trees, cutting up wood, and ripping stumps from the hard ground which encased them, was all a part of a hard day's work.

"It does look lovely," said Henny.

"Look, why don't you take it? Look at it as a favour," said Kasimir.

"Are you sure... that's all; just a savour; from a friend?"

"Of course, my dear Henny. Please, take it, and keep your shawl, too."

"Thank you, Kasimir," said Henny as she took the cheese and brushed past the kapo to head for the parade where roll call was about to commence. "My husband also thanks you. He will be pleased to hear of your hospitality when he returns from the forest."

Kasimir watched as the young woman disappeared from view with his cheese.

"Yes, dear, and I thank you very much, too," he said out loud, though no one could hear, for he was alone at that minute. "You will serve me well."

Kasimir didn't wish to be robbed of the advantage he had found for himself. He wasted no time at all in seeing one of his friends, a guard in charge of the 'tree commando'. His only wish now was for the young man, Henny's husband, to be looked after, not to be beaten; he would take control of the rest. As far as Kasimir was concerned, the husband of Henny's was nothing more than a pawn to him, to be employed as best could be. The husband was his ticket to sexual pleasure, but he must first have a name, and so he goes about his duty and gets the information he needs before confronting his friend, the guard.

CHAPTER 12

Kasimir didn't take long in finding out that Henny's husband's name was Phillipje, and he was even faster to request special favour for him whilst he was attached to the 'tree commando'.

For two days the work in the forest went well for Phillipje and he was oblivious to the fact that he seemed to be left alone most of the time, and so long as he worked hard he seemed to fit in well with the work. He was cursed from time to time but generally speaking was treated with much favour when compared to the other workers.

The work was hard but he seldom got beaten. Beatings for him were rarely seen for he was young and could get the work done, or so he thought; but a guard secretly received cigarettes from Kasimir, for the kapo had eyes for Henny.

The young man toiled away at his hard labour and was oblivious to the good treatment that he received, and failed to see how it was that his wife, so pretty, could provide him with what appeared to be an extra ration of soup each day that he returned to the barracks.

But favours must be rewarded and to this note, the kapo known of Kasimir stirs his caldron well, bringing great joy to the surface.

Kasimir approached Henny in the barracks, pulling the door closed behind him. It was time for roll call and no one else was in the hut.

"I must go, Kasimir," said Henny with fear in her throat. "I have to go outside."

"Not today, Henny," said Kasimir. "I need to talk to you for a minute... just a minute of your time."

"What is it? Is something wrong, perhaps?"

"No, not at all," assured Kasimir. "But I have been a good friend to you and your husband of late."

"Yes, thank you so much," said Henny, still very fearful.

"In fact, the reason your husband comes home to you each day, unbeaten and well fed, to eat more that you can provide him, is for the favours I have been doing you, and now... it is time to collect on those favours."

"What do you mean to say?" asked Henny, knowing full well what was about to occur.

"I like you, Henny; I find you pretty," said Kasimir with a smile, his rotten teeth showing through the grin. "I think you know what I want, and I'll get it, too."

"But I don't want it," said Henny. "I don't want to be friends any more. I can't take your food or hospitality any longer."

"I'm sorry to hear that, Henny. But look at it this way. If I don't get what I want then the extra food will stop, your rations will be less than the others, and your husband will receive beatings and have his rations stopped."

"You can't do that," said Henny.

"Oh, but I can. I was the one that gave you and your husband the fair treatment that you've received so far and I can stop it with a simple whisper in the guards' ears."

"I'm sorry, Kasimir. I don't wish for any more food," and Henny stormed out of the barracks to the roll call.

Kasimir smiled to himself once more. Of course he could have beaten her and had his way, but to have her permission whilst he assaulted her; that's what he craved.

CHAPTER 13

Phillipje was working with the other men of the 'tree commando', doing as they did and not an ounce more. It was a cunning trick that he'd learnt to pull, for he was growing accustomed to the fair treatment, a dangerous trick where he grew lazy and did no more than he felt he should do, a manoeuvre that could see him in big trouble if he was caught. He was fitter and stronger than all the others of the work party and it was because of the extra ration that he received that he fended so well amongst the growing disease of the camp. But the guards had been given the whisper, a message from another guard who had a friend. And so, Phillipje's days were numbered.

"That one, there," said Erik to the corporal in charge. "He's the one."

"Very well," replied the corporal, looking over his back to the sergeant who was out of good visual range; not that it mattered, for the sergeant would take the corporal's word for whatever he said. "We'll punish him and two others; just pick two, it doesn't matter which."

"That one, the one with the scar on his cheek, and the one that limps... he's a lazy bastard, always using his leg as an excuse to slow his work. It's good he gets beatings, but I think it's time he got more – I hunger for a good cigarette."

"Yes, me too," agreed the corporal. "Okay, let's not waste any more time."

Erik strode up to where Phillipje was standing with a smile upon his face, unaware of what was about to happen to him, and the corporal followed close behind. The SS guard saw a dumb reflection in the Jew's eye, but it wasn't that at all, it was the strength of character and the innocence of man that the guard really saw: for it was the guard that was too stupid to know that his sadistic mind was thwart with hidden agendas.

Erik allowed nothing to slip and then without warning he swung his truncheon to strike the prisoner above the knee, careful not to break it, for to do so would see the stream of cigarettes dry up completely; the cigarettes, always the cigarettes; and the cigarettes were his payment for holding his temper. The corporal quickly deposited several portions of a slice of bread upon the ground at Phillipje's feet.

"You damn Jew, I'll kick your useless arse all the way back to camp if you do that again!" yelled Erik.

The sergeant looked over to see what the matter was, seeing Erik with the corporal just behind him.

Phillipje fell to the ground and Erik gave him a swift kick before the corporal rushed in and throttled the two men beside him.

"What is the matter here?" asked the sergeant as he made his way over to the scene in a slow and uncaring manner, not concerned over the beatings that the men were being subjected to but concerned over the unscheduled stop to the work being carried out.

"These men were seen eating bread, sergeant," said the corporal.

The sergeant looked down upon the three men now lying on the ground in pain, each holding their thighs, their faces screwed up.

"Then they deserve more than to have their arses kicked," said the sergeant.

"Permission to string them up, sergeant?" requested the corporal; formerly, knowing full well that permission would be granted.

"Yes; immediately. I won't stand for such ignorance of the system by a pathetic, stinking Jew, in particular one that looks up into my face from there upon the ground. See to it, corporal."

"I didn't do anything," protested Phillipje. This was followed immediately by a flurry of blows from three separate truncheons.

"If you stinking bastards so much as utter a single word of complaint," said the corporal, "then I swear to God, I'll see you shot and strung from the tallest tree, so that the crows can have their way with you."

Nigel B.J. Clayton

One of the Jews, too tired to think straight, too tired to shut his mouth, opened up and voiced his opinion of the guard. "What would you know of God?"

Erik pulled his luger from its holster and waved it in signal for the man to be taken aside.

"It's okay, corporal," said the sergeant. "I'll attend to this one; see the others are strung up."

"Yes, sergeant," and the corporal clicked his heels together in a way of passing a compliment.

A single guard aided the sergeant by following close behind, and with the offender in hand, his arm pushed high from behind, almost tearing it from its socket, the pain written heavily upon the prisoner's face, he was pushed this way and then shoved that.

"God will have his vengeance," said the prisoner between clenched teeth before receiving a swift kick in the guts.

"You get that for free," said the sergeant.

The threesome had gone about three hundred yards into the forest when the sergeant ordered the corporal to stop. The prisoner was pushed to his knees and held in place there for a few moments before being let go.

The sergeant moved to the prisoner's front and placed his boot on the ground. "Lick it clean, Jew."

The prisoner looked up and into the sergeant's eyes, a sparkle within. The sergeant smiled.

"Come on, lick it clean," said the sergeant in a quiet manner. "Your friends aren't here to see you; come on."

The man on his knees commenced licking the entire boot, from sole, to toe, and all the way up to where it finished just below the knee. With the task complete the prisoner withdrew his mouth.

"Now put away your tongue," said the sergeant as he took his luger from its holster and moved behind the man on the ground. "Do you know what is to happen to you; do you know the price for insubordination?"

The prisoner didn't answer and kept looking to his front, knowing full well that he was about to die.

The sergeant pushed the prisoner over, forcing him to the ground with a push with his leg. The prisoner rolled over onto his back and looked up once more and saw the guard's eyes cloud over and his smile evaporate.

"It's good that you can see this coming," said the sergeant, and he pointed his weapon and pulled the trigger.

The shot rang out loud and clear and the Jews all around stopped for a brief second, looking up to see what was going on.

"Get back to work, scum," yelled a guard. "Or you'll be next."

The corporal looked up at his small quarry, the two men he had rounded up for torture. They were both hanging from a tree, by the hands, hands tied together behind their backs. The pain was excruciating.

"You can both wait there," said the corporal with a laugh. "You'll be let down when it's time to go back to the barracks, in an hour."

The man beside Phillipje could take the insult no more and did the unsavoury thing by speaking out.

"Please, I can't take this. I'll do whatever you want. Please let me down... I'll make it worth your while."

The corporal looked at the limp body as it hung from the tree, arms pulled back and held above his head.

"You," said the corporal. "You will stay here all night. I'll cut you down if you're still alive when we get back tomorrow morning," but all knew very well that the man would not survive to see the sun fall beyond the horizon. The agony which he was about to suffer was beyond his wildest imagination.

CHAPTER 14

When Phillipje returned to the barracks, Henny couldn't believe the state he was in. Four prisoners deposited him upon the entrance to the hut. The man who had felt as though he was emancipated, by his luck and good fortune, was now nothing more than a pile of sad refuse upon the floor for all to see. He'd been well and truly tortured, hung from a tree for a full hour, and when it was time to bring him down he was beaten solidly for three or four minutes, every inch of his body being hammered by the guards.

Henny rushed to him and fell in place beside the mass of flesh, hugging and kissing the poor man as he winced in pain from her delicate caresses. The look in his swollen eyes said that he had no idea why this thing was done to him, but she knew why... she knew exactly.

A call then came for each and every one to line up for their meal and Henny fought hard to pull herself from her man, to take her position in the line. She moved forward slowly as each and everyone received their ladle of watery soup and she continued to look over her shoulder, towards where her husband was curled up in pain. She now stood before the kapo.

"You have done a cruel thing, Kasimir," said Henny.

"Maybe you would like some soup," was Kasimir's reply as he scraped the bottom for a good ladle-full of vegetable flesh. He poured it into her bowl. "Some for your husband, perhaps?" Kasimir looked her in the eyes. "It can always be like this, Henny; always plenty to eat... and good treatment for your husband, too."

Henny held out a second bowl, looking from side to side, seeing a few cold stares come her way from the other prisoners.

"You know the price, do you not?" questioned Kasimir quietly.

"I do," replied Henny.

"Good. I shall speak with my friends in the morning. You will be content. Your husband won't be beaten anymore."

And Kasimir saw to it that his promise was carried out for his feelings of lust were deep, and each night, as the ladle was dipped into the watery soup, he managed to retrieve Henny a good portion that was reward for her devotion to him. His ladle now scraped against the bottom in order to get the vegetable flesh into the scoop, and always there was plenty for her, but others in the barrack were annoyed that she was pretty, for they just got the water which was little flavoured and provided no nourishment at all. Phillipje was also treated with great care and so long as he did his job he came back to the hut each night without a mark upon him.

Kasimir appeared at the barracks which stood empty at midday, for roll call had been called. It was time for him to collect his pleasure. He saw the young girl and approached with a smile and she immediately undressed and climbed upon the bunk in order to get the dirty job done. She wanted for her husband to live, for him to go without the beatings, for them both to have a life together in the unforeseen future to come. The only way she could secure this was to surrender to the whims of the kapo. But when the kapo's lust for her died, so too would the favours, and so she would have to give the best performance she could muster, keeping the kapo as happy as he could be kept.

CHAPTER 15

Whilst at duty with the 'shoe commando', Miriam accidentally cut herself upon the wrist with a knife as she carried out her work on a pair of shoes, doing all she could to stay awake, just managing to keep her eyes open by talking freely with those around her, all in the hope that her work would continue as the guards looked around at those under their command. She was now paying for her lapse in concentration, and although the cut didn't penetrate deep it was enough to bring much blood to the cold air, covering her hand and lower arm in seconds; all over her knife and the table top: the blood got everywhere, but the guard was either too ignorant to attend or too stupid to notice that something had happened.

She let out several muffled cries for help and the lady beside her, Hetty, grabbed at a helmet full of cloth and commenced to bandage the wound which was initially seen as quite the threat to life. All of those around continued to work but did so silently, looking upon the unfortunate woman as she tried to help the one that bandaged her.

One of the SS guards in view was finally drawn to the commotion and quickly strutted over with his curiosity entwined with frustration and anger, searching for an explanation for the disturbance. There was work to be done and the last thing the guard wished was for something to go wrong during the course of his duty.

"What is this," he demanded, the intrusion upon his daily choir too much to handle. "What's going on here?"

"Miriam has cut herself," said Hetty, concerned for her friend. Friends were hard to come by, hard to trust, and needed to be held on to for the duration of their unlawful incarceration in Bergen-Belsen.

"Cut herself," stated the guard. "Let me see."

"Here," said Hetty as she pushed Miriam's arm out for the guard to see. "The blood is everywhere. She'll have to see the doctor."

The guard looked at the cut. "You should have your arse kicked all the way back to the barracks for being so careless. I'm tired of you stinking people; it's always something with you. You should be given a good whipping; that's what."

"What's going on?" said another guard as he approached. "What's going on here?"

"This stupid slut, Miriam—," started the guard.

"I don't care what her name is," interrupted the other guard. "What's her number," and laughed out loud at his own joke. "Roll up her sleeve and take a look."

"She's cut herself," repeated the first.

"This miserable piece of shit has tried to commit suicide and failed to achieve a result," came the answer to the concern. "Don't bother yourself with this lazy scum. She's after a day off," the guard looked down upon Miriam as Hetty finished the task of applying a bandage as best she could. "If you wanted to commit suicide then you should have told me. I can help you out; free of charge," and spat upon the woman where she sat. "She'll stay and work like the others," said the guard as he looked his companion in the eye. "Ensure she does her share," and he walked off, shaking his head.

The first guard remained in place. "You stupid slut; what are you about? Do you want me to look like a fool? I'm tired of being nice to you. You will get your work done, like the others, and if I find that your quota has been neglected then I shall see you all standing at the fence for the entire night."

Hetty continued to tie the bandage in place for Miriam as the work around them continued and the guard moved away.

"You will have to take care of your injury," said Hetty. "You aren't going to get any favours here. Get some rest tonight, Miriam."

Miriam looked after the guard as he continued to assess the work further down the table. "Who is he, so high and mighty; what favour has he done us? I've had nothing to eat except dry cabbage in water for two days running, treated like a slave, spoke to like an animal, and he says he's tired of being nice."

"Don't let him trouble you, Miriam. He'll hear you," said Hetty.

"And when he does we'll all be punished for your stupidity," said one of the women from across the table, angered that Miriam should jeopardise her safety.

CHAPTER 16

Even now, the introduction of three-tiered bunks was prominent in most parts of the camp, in particular where the former stables had been arranged in quarters for one faction of prisoner, mattresses so thin that they couldn't be accounted for anything, nothing more than bedding enough for the bugs of the night which would choose to come out by dark for their chance of something to eat.

Ashamed the prisoners all were in such dilapidated conditions that it never even entered their minds that conditions could get much worse.

The stables consisted of four quarters with three toilets and a washing shed; it was a sheer pity that the toilets often became clogged with faeces that, given time, the inmates en mass would simply shrug their shoulders and await as patiently as possible in line for their turn at the one which was in good working order, or simply employ the hollowed out space of a jug or vase which could be emptied at its earliest convenience. Such were the rudiments of life here that little decorum of any description was seen, and shitting was a daily choir.

There was no respectability in standing within line and awaiting your turn to use the toilet when, with the expulsion of gas from within, the remnants of the meagre meals consumed during the day, came gushing out and quite often down the legs.

"Olga; where are you going?" asked Sarah as she gently grabbed hold of her friend's arm. "There are only a few people in front of you now."

Olga looked to the front of the line and towards the toilet; she then looked down upon the ground.

Sarah followed her glance and saw the shit as it pooled around her friend's feet, the smell going unnoticed for the stench in the barracks was much the same no matter where you went.

"Don't let it get you down, Olga," encouraged Sarah. "It has happened to all of us."

"Yes, I know," said Olga with a tempted smile. "I need my

rest. I'm going to try and clean myself and then go to sleep."

"Won't you stay up until the soup arrives?"

"That's why I shit so much," replied Olga. "I'm too tired. I have to sleep."

"You take care, Olga," insisted Sarah. "You're my good friend. I don't want to see you too depressed. I'll wake you when the soup arrives."

"Thank you, Sarah; you're a good friend," said Olga one last time and disappeared towards her bunk where she would have to climb up two tiers and over at least one person, for there was always someone laying down in sickness and poor health.

By the time Olga had gotten to her bunk she could see that two were asleep at the top. She reached up and grabbed a small piece of cloth that hung upon a nail, her cleaning rag. She took it and moved over towards the washing shed where she'd hoped to be able to get some water. She was in luck.

She took her pyjama trousers off and stood there with nothing on but a worn shirt. Several men could be seen going about their business but she was unashamed, as anyone else was in this camp of filth. She scrubbed hard the thin fabric and tried with all her strength to get the stain from within the pyjamas to wash away. After a few minutes she had attained a reasonable amount of success and so placed the trousers back on and decided on a quick look outside to help them dry upon her legs.

The night was very cold and she shivered there, wondering what it would be like to have something better to eat; somewhere nicer to sleep.

Several towers could be easily seen from where she stood and the guards in these continued their watch, studying their area of responsibility, ensuring that no prisoner went near a fence they weren't supposed to approach, or speak with anyone that it was forbidden to speak with.

Olga had heard that family and friends were prevalent in the camp, that one member from one area within the camp would endeavour to push a potato or turnip through the wire so that another could share in their fortunate lives, for not all in Bergen-

Belsen were treated as heavy-handily as another.

As she stood there watching she noticed that there was a child wandering about, a stray child having wandered too far from its hut and seemingly looking for its mother. And as she continued to watch, she saw an adult come out of hiding, walking in a mild rush towards the infant which couldn't have been more than three to four years of age.

"Hey, what are you doing?" yelled Olga, forgetful.

The guard in the nearest tower looked down upon her, thinking her suspicious.

"Who goes there?" yelled the guard, the beam of his searchlight falling upon her. "What are you doing near the fence?"

"I saw something," yelled Olga in reply. "A child."

"Stay away from the fence," yelled the guard. "Stay where you are, someone will be there shortly, you nosey, Jew-bitch."

Olga looked over and could just barely see that the figure of a woman had reached the child and had picked it up.

"No; there she is," and Olga ran towards the fence.

"Halt!" yelled the guard, and the next moment he fired his rifle and Olga fell down dead.

The other woman halted and looked over her shoulder before returning to her task and carried the child to safety.

She placed the child down out of view from the tower.

"What's your name?" she asked.

The boy was scared, scared to death, but he knew that he was in a camp for unfortunates, kept locked away against his free will, even though he didn't know what 'free will' was.

"Abraham," said the little child in a whisper.

"Well, Abraham; I'm Annie," replied the adult. "Are you alone?" and she knew he was, for she'd seen his mother die.

"My mummy has gone," said Abraham with tears in his eyes.

"Do you know that you shouldn't be near the fence? You'll be shot... dead," she wished to scare the child more than anything else. Her own child had died just that morning and she was without her reason for being tended to like a good little lamb. Whilst she remained with a child she was fed better than the others, and with a child so young she was advantaged by not having to go to work.

"I miss my mother."

"I know you do, Abraham," said Annie. "But we have to help each other now. But you have to listen to me closely; very closely. If you want to stay alive then you have to pretend, Abraham, and we don't have much time."

"Why?" asked Abraham.

"Don't worry about that right now," said Annie. "Just listen to me, and listen carefully. The nasty men that watch us day and night; they will take you away if they find you without a mother, do you understand?"

"Yes," replied Abraham.

"Good; now listen to me... your name isn't Abraham anymore, you hear? Your name is Max."

"I don't like Max," said Abraham.

"You have no choice, Max. You have to be, or they'll take you away and kill you."

"I wasn't naughty, I wasn't bad," said Abraham. "I just want my mother," and he sobbed too loudly for Annie's comfort.

She picked him up and scurried away to her hut, the child in her arms. "I'll look after you, Max; you're my son now. We'll look after each other. How does that sound; uh?"

"Will I see my mother again?"

"No, Max; you won't; but together we can live," explained Annie, and both mother and child disappeared into the darkness, one in the arms of the other.

CHAPTER 17

Sarah felt poorly that her friend was dead. One moment she was standing in the line for the ablutions and the next, she had a hole in her head. Those bastard SS were good shots with the rifle, there was no doubt about that. With camp life came much practice for the guards to hone their shooting skills. There was a great injustice about it all, how the SS seemed to think it was all a game, how the mistreatment of the Jews below them would somehow see them be honoured with the presentation of an Iron Cross for a job well done.

Sarah had realised rather quickly, that although she felt for her dead friend, Olga, her own life was more important. It was like having to choose which child was next to be shot: would it be one from her extended family, or the boy in the next barracks? The choice was easy. Life was precious, and no more precious was it than to the person who held it most dearly – the individual.

The following night's meal was the same as the night before, which was the same again for every night that past fortnight: from what she could recall. She was so tired that she rarely knew what was real and what was not; it was all like a dream to her.

She received her ladled water where several green pieces of something could be seen floating on the surface: a little lettuce, perhaps. Her eyes grew wide, just for a small piece of lettuce; she was going crazy with hunger.

Someone looked over to Sarah as she held the bowl to her lips – no one bothered to use spoons any more – and from the corner of her eye, Sarah could see the woman lick her lips. If Sarah was to fall dead that minute her bowl would be emptied faster than she would hit the floor in a spasm of death.

The woman's name was unknown to Sarah but it was obvious she wished to take more than she was welcome to. Sarah would, from this day forth, keep an eye open for the evil looking cow now watching her. Everybody had enemies; everyone wanted extra food to eat.

The kapo of the hut was far too mean to issue a proper portion to those under his care; it was the sex he cared about more than anything else. The kapo was nothing more than a criminal, so why should he be in charge? Then again, the SS were no different, a bunch of criminals who saw it as their duty to torture and kill.

Sarah continued to drink from her bowl and closed her eyes as the watery soup went down her throat. Her throat was a little sore but she wouldn't waste anything that she was given to eat or drink. In her imagination she could swear that she could taste carrots. Maybe the kapo rubbed the inside of the kettle with some carrot juice before it was delivered to her bowl, to tease her imagination, to drive her further into insanity than she had already fallen. It was then that her eyes flew wide open, as she reached the bottom of her bowl, for there was at least a large spoonful of vegetable matter at the bottom. She had struck it rich.

Ah, the delectable taste and texture of real food; it was beyond imagination; it was sheer luxury; and the soup was warm, also. Maybe the kapo was after her body, she thought.

A call suddenly erupted throughout the barracks, the entire camp called to roll call. It was dark outside and freezing, no place for a human being.

The rain was coming down in buckets, no reprieve for those making their way out onto parade, to be lined up in five ranks, covered off from front to rear. It took rather a while before everyone was in position and the guards made their way through the huts, counting all of those with a doctor's order to stay in bed.

The SS corporal came storming out of the hut from behind Sarah.

"There's a body in the hut, you filth-mongers," yelled the guard. "You and you; get your filthy arses inside and drag it out; now!"

Sarah turned around having not seen that she was one of those ordered to duty.

"You better be deaf," said the corporal as he lifted his truncheon and smashed it into her face, knocking out all of her teeth, "you stupid, lazy bitch. Get off your knees and to work; I have no need for my boots to be cleaned. It's raining you stupid cow; move it!"

Sarah had no use for tears; they'd been used up long ago. Here she was on her knees, her teeth knocked out and swallowed up by the mud of the parade as the rain continued to fall without remorse.

Sarah got up and followed the other person into the hut; it was Olga.

"Olga, my dear friend," said Sarah. "You've come back."

"Stop your talking," said the corporal and gave her a shove from behind.

Sarah fell forward, into the mud once more, and into the person in front of her.

"Olga, help me," said Sarah as she looked up from the mud at the foot of the steps into the hut. "Help me, Olga."

The woman looked down upon Sarah and then to the corporal. "I don't know what she's saying. I'm not Olga."

"Shut your mouth," said the guard. "You go and get the body by yourself and deposit it in the gutter... you can take care of it in the morning."

The corporal looked down upon the smiling Sarah, and she looked up with arms held out for Olga, her dearest friend.

The corporal swung his truncheon from high to low, bringing it down hard and upon Sarah's outstretched arms. Both snapped, heard over the roar of the rain.

Sarah sank further into the mud and the corporal beat down upon the woman until she was dead by bashing, or by drowning in the mud, either way the guard couldn't care less. To the guard she was nothing more than a stinking Jew, another number, another animal amongst animals which deserved to be beaten.

Senior Sergeant Weingartner, the blockführer, moved over to where the corporal was standing.

"She'd gone mad," said the corporal, "a lunatic."

"She got what she deserved," said the sergeant. He looked down upon the back of the dead woman and noticed the legs of the one beside her. She'd pissed herself, the steam of the urine erupting from the pyjamas like the vapours from a volcano.

"Trying to keep warm, are you?" asked the sergeant sarcastically. "Look at me when I speak, whore-bag."

The woman looked at the sergeant, shaking from the cold of the night, the rain continuing to fall upon them all.

The sergeant lifted his whip and placed it under her chin. "If you were 40 pounds heavier you might be worth something. Get your scrawny arse over to the fence and stay there until you're relieved of your punishment."

As the woman moved away the sergeant addressed the parade. "Anyone else wishing to defile this ground may do so, but next time I shall not be so lenient. Corporal."

"Yes, sergeant."

"See to it that the woman remains at the fence until first light."

"Yes, sergeant."

CHAPTER 18

It was an underestimate to assume that several thousand bombers had flown overhead during February, overhead the camp during nights which allowed for good visual recognition of targets, the number in all reality being a lot more than an inmate's imagination could commit to. It got the strength of the poor souls up, those relinquished to the cruelty of the SS feeling an emotion of happiness within them, their confidence soaring high on wings-of-a-prayer, for it all meant that the war was nearing its end; there was simply no other explanation. The very thought of the war ending ripped the prisoners from the brink of their despair, even if for a short time only.

The commandant was quick to see that the planes could easily cause quite the headache, and in particular was the threat of a ground assault upon his very camp; but he had considered that the allies wouldn't dare assault a prisoner of war camp, let alone a camp full of pathetic Jews, the source of his aggravation. He hated them all with such great passion that if the same amount of passion was to be consumed writing a sonnet or similar, it would be remembered as the greatest gift to mankind, ever.

Kramer ordered that a work party be organised for the defences of the camp to commence. He ordered that a trench be dug for the protection of the SS and this was to be dug with the prisoner's food bowls – why on earth would he wish to provide them with tools? The task was insane and served no purpose, but it did provide the commandant with feelings of joy, to see that he held much power and influence over those he called 'scum'.

The weather had not improved much over the past few weeks and the ground was back-breaking hard from the cold nights. A little snow could be seen to fall from the sky, through dirty and broken panes, looked upon by wandering eyes as they perused the surroundings for answers.

When would the war end? When would the torture stop? When would the tormentors receive just punishment? They were questions that had no answer for a lot of the people in Bergen-

Belsen, for a lot of those in this place of hell would be dead before salvation could be granted.

A mysterious hand rubbed a clear space upon a window pane, to attain a clearer view of what was happening outside. Different parts of the camp could be seen from this single vantage point. There were so many different nationalities here that had it easier than others, and most of it stemmed from whether or not you were a prisoner of war or a Jew whose arse was marked with a big red 'X'.

Most of the 'Exchange Jews' were seen to wear a visible yellow star sewn upon their lapel or breast and although a prisoner uniform (pyjamas) were worn by many, a majority of these favourites wore civilian clothing. The last thing the SS wanted was for poor propaganda to escape to the West, but it was too late to worry about such things, for news travelled quickly; this was why those that were classified as 'exchange Jew' were treated better than all the others. But the condition of the camp was not widely known to the rest of the world in the present moment, and this was a good thing for the SS, and could only help the German cause as opposed to ruin it.

A SS guard moved between two watch towers, moving steadily upon his feet with a leash in his hand. He carried a rifle upon his shoulder, attached by its strap, and the German Sheppard was controlled well by him as they both moved up and down their responsibility. It was their duty to ensure that no conversation between prisoners, from one compound to the next, was shared. 'Exchange Jews' could not be permitted to depart the camp of horror with dirty laundry sewn within their lips.

The entire camp was surrounded by a double fence of barbed wire and not a second went by where there was not a single metre of ground that was not covered by German eyes. Armed guards and dogs; more dogs and their handlers; rifles loaded and ready to use; there was simply no escape.

The hard labour of digging a trench under Kramer's order continued for many days and men were whipped and beaten, punched and kicked, kicked and scolded. Everyone was treated like an animal, but some animals received fairer treatment than others.

Eventually the work was done and the trench was finished. It was now time to inspect the work carried out by the prisoners.

Kramer looked over the work which had been done and was pleased that it had been carried out as per his orders, but he had had a change of mind, and so, two weeks after the trenches had been ordered dug, he ordered them filled.

Only a lunatic could cause such pain to be forced upon many prisoners, day after day, after day, all held against their will, but it takes a highly motivated lunatic to run a concentration camp.

CHAPTER 19

In the early days of camp life it was seldom seen that a person, as an individual, would be confronted with the horrors of death. If death occurred then it was a sad occasion, in particular for family and friends – where such existed. And it was always good to have friends, in particular towards the end of the war, for when the time of Hitler's downfall was upon them all it was good to have someone close to the breast that would die for your cause; and many people in the insanity of camp life wished for heavier clothing to stave off the cold, and clothing could most favourably be obtained from the dead. A dead person had no need for clothing or food and no sooner did someone pass away and their personal belongings were confiscated quick-smart by those who knew the person best. There was no reading of wills necessary, just quick hands and fast minds.

As time passed, so did the occurrences of death. What was rarely seen was now a part of everyday life. Day in and day out, night after night; someone would die, their bodies would be stripped, their belongings dissolved; and where the fortunate were concerned, death showered them with great respect, for the deceased were thrown into the gutter to be picked up later, not to be shoved under the floorboards and forgotten. Such were the advantages of friendship that to be placed in the gutter was a mark of respect, for it meant twice the handling and a possible service when the dead were collected the following morning.

Something of a horrid nature was then brought to air, for someone had stolen a loaf of bread from the kitchen. For this a punishment would be issued to the entire camp, for one mans' crime was for all to share.

Everyone was to stand on parade, to stand there in the snow, and for nine hours be subjected to the freezing wind and white specks of ice that fell from the sky. Kapos were placed in charge, ordered to watch over those on parade, and from high in the towers along the barbed wire fence the ever watchful eyes of the guards looked upon everyone to ensure that nothing and no one fell out of place.

The kapos had little choice but to suffer the weather as did the inmates, but the kapos had something to keep them warm: the beating of those before them.

The exercise of beating old men and women provided the kapos with the opportunity to maintain their warmth throughout the hours that they had to stand there, taking time off now and again for a drink of water or something small to eat.

By the time it was over and the punishment was seen to fit the crime, rations were stopped for two days and everyone was fallen out to move back to their huts and continue with their horrible lives in unsanitary conditions.

A man was laying half frozen on the ground, exposed to the open air, stepped over by hundreds of inmates as they moved into warmer surroundings. It was freezing cold, so cold that it was unimaginable how the man was still alive. He held up his hand for help, hoping for someone to pick him up and carry him inside, but he was heavy and everyone else was tired. Each and every one needed to conserve their energy for the loved ones in their life, not to be tied down by attending to an old man. Give an inch and he would take a mile. Help him now and he would return to be helped again, and again, and again later on. It simply couldn't be permitted to happen.

The old man's feet felt as though they were frozen, frozen solid, and he couldn't move. The pain was too great, the infliction beyond contemplation.

And the horrors of the night were as bad as those by day, where lice and bed bugs had their way upon every person and if an individual was unlucky, an inmate from the bunk above would shit on their head.

Such was life in this place.

Sonja got up and took her place in line for the toilet. She was fortunate this morning because there were not many in the queue. Most were too sick to move, or too tired to get up, which was unfortunate for the sanitary conditions of the hut, for almost everyone had diarrhoea.

Sonja moved into the toilet and there she found a dead body, an elderly lady, dead upon the toilet seat, sitting there having relieved her bowels but dying before given the chance to wipe her own arse. What an unforgiving position this was.

But the pity she felt for the deceased was superseded by her own need to relieve herself and so she sat upon the bare porcelain just in time. Her bowels emptied, like running water from a tap. She had now done her morning duty, but she was still sitting there when an old man then came and sat beside her, and did as he needed to do on another. There was no shame felt, no discomfort in the situation, for they shared a common misery and the last thing on their mind was to show any decency whilst shitting: and all before the dead was removed from her place upon the bar.

Finally it was time to move, time to get ready for the morning's roll call. She got to her feet and was about to remove herself from the stench of her surroundings when a sudden felt urge fell upon her. She felt disgusted in herself for not having helped the dead woman. The least she could do was place her outside so that she could receive a cremation – even if cremation might not be granted, for there were a hell of a lot of bodies mounting up outside.

Sonja heaved and jerked and pulled with all her strength, doing all she could to remove the body of the dead woman. The man on the toilet that sat next to her was still sitting, looking upon her as though thinking how stupid she was to be wasting her time with such a foolish errand.

Inch by inch, the body was dragged along the floor, picking up faeces as she was pulled, literally cleaning the excrement that was evident upon the floorboards of their shitting quarters. She continued to pull and finally came to the door where all that was left of Sonja's energy was enough to push the remains with her foot into the cold morning air. Across from her was a pile of dead, and it grew in height, length and width, and deposited there were those that had been erased from the face of the world, to be lost forever of human contact.

The body fell away from the step and Sonja looked to the side. There she saw an old man, frozen stiff from the night before, unable to extricate himself from his position. Why hadn't someone helped him?

Sonja looked up again, further afield. The cart was coming, the cart with a body upon it, and she could see the small crowd of people as they watched it being pulled along, and she could hear the comments of the SS guard on duty.

This was the parade of the dead, a ceremony so often seen, witnessed more and more as the days went by. A family member had died and was thrown upon a cart to be wheeled away to the pile of stench and decaying corpses: this was the 'death cart'. The recently deceased loved one received a few shed tears and when a young one had passed away the tears and sobs were heavier and the sadness more terrible. There was no decent burial to speak of. And as the cart was wheeled away by several weak men, so crippled with disease that it was hard to stay on two feet, the SS guard puffed on a cigarette and passed an unfavourable comment upon the poor teenager that was alive just the night before.

"You stinking Jews, always wasting your time. If you have strength to cart away the body then you have time to work. Yes; you three; report to me when your job is done. I'll put you to work, licking my boots clean," the sergeant looked to the sobbing few that watched the cart being pulled away. "I have shit all over my boots; it's your shit and you can have it back, you pathetic scum of a race." The sergeant drew on his cigarette and seemed drunk with power, and looked again to the cart being pulled along slowly. "I had my way with that one. Squirm, she did, and all for the price of a slice of bread. You filthy swine make me puke... imagine that; selling your virginity for a slice of bread."

And the mother could only cry for her daughter, a final touch in farewell, her hand touching the arm of the deceased. Her mother could easily forgive her daughter's encounter with the sergeant, for in essence it was of no issue at all, but the sergeant;

such hatred for these swine of men she held within her that she would never forget them, never forgive.

CHAPTER 20

American planes zoomed overhead and engaged a target some distance away, plumes of smoke eventually being seen as they encrusted the clear sky. It was amazing that such an event could bring so much joy to a person, and so much fear, too; both at the same time.

The inmates feared that the machine gun fire from the aircraft would indiscriminately target them, bullets sprayed from a barrel finding themselves falling amongst the throng as they watched with their hands on their hearts, praying to be delivered from the hellhole known as Bergen-Belsen.

Every single person felt the uplifting spirit within them, the sheer jubilance that the war could be approaching something of an end, a most favourable outcome for their situation, where weeks or years of being treated like an animal had been suffered, different stints of time being drawn upon each of those held against their will.

If the allies were so close to concern themselves with engaging targets around the camp then the fight must surely have been in the allies favour. And then a little pessimism, too, entered their minds, for they needed to also consider that this might simply be a single engagement where targets behind enemy lines were more readily hit with little retaliation, an incursion deep into hostile territory which amounted to fewer casualties of their own being suffered.

Again the planes flew overhead, and whether or not they were the same ones or not, the onlookers did not know, but they scrambled into the gutter alongside the street when the firing got too close for comfort, where SS guards had also buried their faces. Both prisoner and guard were now alongside the other, and it seemed, somehow, just a dream. So briefly did the inmates feel as though they were one and the same, joined together in misery, and then the feelings of despair and hatred for these devil worshippers hit them hard once more, for no other than a devil worshipper could inflict such heinous acts of criminal

Niꞔel B.J. Clayton

injustice upon the weak and meek.

Air raids by day and by night; again the feelings of joy and fear erupt from within. It was all possible that a bomb could fall upon the huts in the dark. But the knowledge that the allies were advancing upon the enemy that imprisoned them all was a savour in the face of the doom that surrounded the innocent, and enlightened everyone to the streaks of yellow grime that were painted upon the backs of those wearing the SS symbol upon their collar, for deep down they were nothing other than cowards, one and all.

It was absurdly amazing, that with all the contempt and punishment that the SS forced upon the inmates, that a single truth, in a majority of the cases, did come of fruition: that a single guard, regardless of the symbol upon his collar, could not beat the weak into submission, for the weak were too strong of heart to give in to those so easily swayed by the devil himself. It was far easier to give in to the Devil than it was to follow a religion; the Jews were strong.

And then a daydream hit Franzi like a fallen brick upon the head. She thought she could see that one of the SS looked familiar, like a husband to a friend she once knew. And then it struck her hard. These SS were fundamentally recruited from those husbands so drunk with power that they felt it their duty to punch and kick and maim their wives as though a common dog, but instead of wives they beat Jews. She; Franzi; was an animal in their eyes, for whatever reason she did not know, treated with no respect whatsoever, maintained like cattle on a farm for the purpose of hard labour and exchange, like currency. She was a commodity. Each and every one of them was a commodity through and through, a bargaining chip, a piece of meat, collateral (though worthless), and like the shit that one wipes from the bottom of his or her shoe they existed in great numbers and were everywhere.

She shook her head and forced the wretched fantasy from within, the thoughts of despair that were starting to strangle them all. They were human beings and deserved as much as any other, to be treated with the respect they deserved. She'd done nothing to deserve this treatment, as had none of them.

The air raids continued well into the week and became second nature, a formality which disturbed the nights and days, the sirens penetrating Franzi's weary bones. Now that she was starting to get used to the sirens and bombs, the episodes of fear that once struck her were beginning to abate, and only the joy she hid within her provided great hope for the future. But the feelings were kept so well hidden, even from conversation, for the last thing she needed was to anger a guard, or one of those under his charge: the stinking kapos.

CHAPTER 21

It was March and the turnips kept on coming.

There was a call for some work to be done as many bags of turnips had arrived. These dirty vegetables needed to be peeled and cut up before being turned into the kitchen kettles. The work was laborious to say the least but there was consolation at the end of the day, for all of those working on the turnips would receive an extra litre of turnip soup at the end of the day's work.

It was a small savour, this extra soup, for the meals were scanty at best: turnips, soup, and a piece of bread if they were lucky. The meal times were now almost non-existent. The guards didn't care whether the prisoners ate or not, let alone drop dead from hunger: one less mouth to feed.

The fat German whores, SS guards one and all, who feed their hungry mouths like pigs at a trough, stood over the weak like the men, and they looked as hard as nails, but are, in the reality of it all, sluts one and the same. There was no real delicate word for these daughters of bitches – the whole damn German race deserved to be annihilated for what they had done: first World War one, and now this madness.

One of the wives saved a few shreds of turnip for her husband who had been suffering badly in the forest, cutting up wood for the stoves of the kitchen, and no doubt, the fire in which the commandant used to keep warm at night when eating a thick steak – no turnips for him.

Her poor husband found it hard to turn out a full day's work in accordance with the guard's wishes, for this was the 'tree commando', which meant hard labour and hard rules. It was here that he was beaten, along with many others, beaten senseless and without good cause: but then again, there never was a good cause for beating a prisoner. If he could just stay ahead, just a little, the others would receive the beating and he would go unscathed. But he was lucky, lucky because many men and women suffered from something, be it a hernia, angina pectoris, diabetes, tuberculosis, starvation, diarrhoea, spotted fever, typhus, typhoid, influenza, gastro-enteritis, scabies, bronco-pneumonia, pressure sores, suppurating wounds, gangrene, or some other ailment: there was a list that kept on growing by the day.

This was the way the system worked; allow your friend and comrade to take the beating in order for you to survive. It was a sorrowful affair, wishing another to take a beating in place of you, but it was the only way to survive, and so if you see your brother taking a hiding you simply shut your mouth and continue with your work, because you had a duty to fulfil in regards to your younger sister, to ensure she survived this horror camp as best she could, or that your wife or child didn't get called out in front of a parade and whipped for the good of nothing.

Ah; those blessed aircraft overhead. The war would surely be over soon for the aircraft overhead appeared frequently and the front line could be heard as it advanced a little each day, in particular at night when there was a strong wind from the west.

From the hour that they were marched into the forest by the guards, where their dogs endeavoured to take a bite of a prisoner from time to time, the SS guards putting strain on the long chains, until the time the workers were marched back, there was no real relent in sight.

It was said by many of the men that the guards seemed quite content to beat them senseless as it was a means by which to keep them warm, but with the approach of warmer weather the beatings for warmth were replaced by more beatings because Germany was losing the war. The inmate never wins; was always a prisoner, always a slave, always the Jew who didn't deserve to be free; an animal to be penned up for ever and a day.

Suddenly there was a call for some men to come running, for a stump needed to be removed post-haste, and the thoughts that run through a man's mind during such hard labour were suddenly washed away, for now was the time to ensure that extra beatings were held at bay.

"You ten men, there," shouted a corporal. "And you lot... get to task – move it!"

The twenty men moved as fast as they could and the stump came into view. It was reasonably small and couldn't possibly be attended to by so many. Too many men in such a small amount of space would impede the work. Who's to work and who's to watch? To stand back and watch was cause to be beaten, beaten to within an inch of your life, and so the men fight each other for the task, pushing one another out of the way in order to get their hands dirty on a job that they didn't have the energy to do. Damned if you did and damned if you didn't, and with that came the rain of blows as several guards moved in with truncheons and started hitting the men over the head.

Blood covers the truncheons in seconds and then another guard moves in with a short whip, letting loose with the power of his arm, metering out his punishment against those getting in the way of the work, and it takes almost a minute of beatings to disperse the men, two of which have died. Punishment for the others was now dealt out which consisted of solitary work upon some of the hardest to move stumps in the vicinity. They would work until they dropped and when they dropped they were beaten once more for being lazy.

A man was almost strangled to death by his own scarf, held up between two guards who had fun tormenting the inmate for not working fast enough, and Phillipje felt sorry for him, but to feel sorry for another was a lasting mistake; wasn't it enough that he was already covered in blood, from head to toe, simply because the guards turned on him like rabid dogs? He stared in error and the guards pounced on him one last time – and it was, indeed, the last time.

But by nightfall the work was done and the bodies of the two dead men were dumped nearby, left for the insects and scavengers of the night to do with as they saw fit.

Henny awaited the return of her husband but he didn't come back and she learns of his death whilst he was at work in the forest. She now fell out of favour with the kapo, Kasimir Cegielski, and the kapo wasn't pleased at all. He finds reason to have her punished and she is later sent to the bunker where she is savaged by dogs under the guise of Irma Grese who had made a name for herself by early March.

Irma Grese, a new arrival, the most notorious after Kramer and only 22 years old. She was the senior supervisor at Auschwitz until January 1945, and returned to Ravensbrück before being dispatched with her hunger for torture to Bergen-Belsen in March. She had an appetite for cruelty and sexual excesses; she was sadistic in her beatings of women with her plaited whip, whipping them until they were dead, and the arbitrary shooting of prisoners came without good reason, and she loved to see her half-starved dogs savage a prisoner. She wore heavy boots and carried a whip and a pistol, used physical and emotional torture, and enjoyed killing in cold blood. But her piece of resistance was her lampshades, made from the skin of three prisoners which she kept in her hut. If the devil had a wife then she was it.

The kapo cared little and now searched for another victim, another young girl to make him happy, but it was hard to find the right one because to him they were mostly ugly; mostly too thin and diseased.

CHAPTER 22

The crematorium had folded, there was no more trying to cope with the mounting dead. There were up to 500 deaths a day now. The burning of the dead was a pointless task and the effort was as futile as a man pissing in a gale whilst trying to fill a cup at his feet. But smoke continued to pour from its chimney, the insanity of the futile task simply too ridiculous to comprehend. Hour after hour it continued to burn without end, the stench of the burning mingling with the rotting corpses that were piling higher and higher.

By the end of March there had been around 18,000 deaths in the entire camp; almost 200 amongst those whom had special treatment; such a small number in comparison, and a true indication as to how better off some of the inmates had it when compared to others, but the right to exist had to be looked upon as being shared by all, not just those of special interest: and what was it to be 'special' in any case? It didn't take a special person to wish for the end of the war. So many wished to see the war end and enjoy the comforts of life once again.

So many people died during the night and it wasn't until morning that they were dragged outside to be piled alongside the others who had died. The piles were growing at an alarming rate. The bodies were ransacked of all their clothing, their shoes, their possessions, and so mostly decomposed naked, rotting into the soil, to become food for the worms and maggots – there was no honour in death; not here.

If the dead had occupied a bunk the position was soon taken by the living and anything of value that might be there was used to the best of the ability of the one that had absconded with it.

Nothing would be left unattended for long; nothing would be left to fall by the wayside; everything had dozens of eyes holding to it, ready to steal for the sake of bartering for food. Everything in the camp had a use and was worth something, be it a kerchief, a spoon, a bowl, or a piece of cloth to wrap your head in; everything was worth something.

Shoes in particular were always an item of great value for no one in the entire camp, apart from those that sat upon the watchtowers with guns, had seen a good pair of shoes for almost two years. It was survival, and the fittest had the advantage. The weak would be dead soon enough and so why waste one's energy in trying to save the dead? It was everyone for himself and only where family was concerned did matters of survival spread from one person to another... but then, not even family could sway the minds of the few, for life had different values for some when compared to others, and it was easy for the torments of the camp to turn good men into degenerated bastards.

Bread ration was reduced to less than a slice a day and the soup was nothing more than water with a few signs of something floating in it, be it spittle from a SS guard, one of the kapos, or the greatest gift of all, a maggot on which to chew. And this was all that was fed to the multitudes, the 44,000 odd prisoners that made up the stench of the camp. And then the inmates' eyes opened in impossible wonder, as another truck made its way into the camp to offload more prisoners.

The meals were a far cry from what could surely be considered as luxurious, but here in Bergen-Belsen, a piece of rotten fruit was a gift from heaven, and three pints of turnip soup per day along with 200 grams of black bread was better than a poke in the eye with a stick.

A wife hid a small portion of soup under her bed, keeping it safe for her husband. A kapo came in and saw her acting suspiciously. He found the soup and threw it over her face, the bowl he confiscated. There was no justice. She broke down crying after he had left the barracks. Life seemed so pointless. It was too hard to survive. If the war didn't end soon then their lives would be no longer.

Work in the kitchen was looked upon as a great favour now, but individuals weren't picked by guards or even kapos, the individuals, instead, would literally fight over the right to work. For the sake of getting their hands on a mug of soup and the opportunity to bite into the hard core of a turnip, or the skin of a

Nl B.J.Clayton

potato, came a mass of women, all screaming for the same job.
They pushed each other and showed no mercy or leniency towards one another. It was here that each and every woman was fighting her way into the kitchen, and each was of equal status, and in a vast majority of cases the women were squabbling for the right to provide something extra, no matter how small, for their husband or child: it mattered little, for everyone was under-nourished or put to heavy work cutting wood in the 'tree commando'.

Yes; a wife felt so compelled to work for the extra food that she'd do anything for it, even to go as far as stab her long-time friend in the back by making out that she'd committed some small crime in order for her to be made to stand at the fence or be denied a job. Sometimes it backfires and the accused is dragged away to the bunker or worse – could there possibly be worse?

They shoved and kicked, elbowed and kicked, punched and pulled and pushed; there was no decorum, no restraint. A shot rang out and a body fell to the ground, the pushing and shoving stopped momentarily and then continued. There was no stopping the mayhem, each and every one of these women was desperate to get an extra cup of soup, and the struggle continued along with a few arrests until the doors were shut because the positions were filled and the bodies that lay dead upon the ground were carried away by the order of the guards.

Other work parties were created, more work for over a thousand women, but this work was not heavily sought for there was no just reward in the form of food. The work was ridiculous, the most ridiculous so far, and not a single one of the multitudes that were forced to gather and work could comprehend what the hell was going on, but one woman heard that the source of their hours of labour was to be used in German war planes.

And what was the insanity? These women were to plait cellophane.

The Third Reich was surely on the brink of surrender. The money-saving choirs in the camp of cellophane plaiting, shoe cutting and the building of more barracks by the hands of those imprisoned, buildings which had no windows, leaking roofs and three-tiered bunks to house the thousands of prisoners still arriving, barracks being built that were little better than tents and the only benefit was for the lice and bed bugs which found the accommodation extremely rewarding and in easy reach of the skin that they get their teeth into.

This was a nightmare come true. And over the coming weeks there was seen to be more and more people subjecting themselves to having their hair cut short in order to keep the lice away, but it did no good and the infestations found harbour in armpits and crotches. Some mad inmates prefered to keep the lice for the sake of looking normal with a head of hair. There were mixed emotions. One would say that if sanity could be maintained for resembling something human then that was good. To feel human meant life, to be insane meant death. Only the strength of body and mind would survive. And so the sane and insane keep their hair for different reasons; the insane did not know the difference and the sane for no other purpose than to remain in control of their meagre possession which would grow back eventually if cut in any case.

Life was ridiculous and unfair.

CHAPTER 23

Work in the kitchen wasn't just about peeling spuds or turnips, but other duties would be performed and some of these tasks had to be tackled early.

Woken at 2:30am; at work in the kitchen by 3:15am. Less than one percent of the total in Bergen-Belsen were expected to perform kitchen duties for the masses.

The kitchen was a mass of kettles; these were what turned out the watery soup, many times in a single day, for there were many barracks and prisoners that needed to be fed an unappetizing mixture of water and water, with water added for flavour.

Rinse the kettles, hose them out, fill them up, stir them well, deliver them to their stations and return the empty kettles back to the kitchen before starting all over again. If there was a break in the day then the prisoners were fortunate, but from the hard work a single consolation was attained: they were permitted to eat as much as they wanted... but how much turnip and water could one person possibly stomach?

It was impossible to imagine the effect that getting dressed so early in the morning could have on a person, in particular where there was human shit all over the floor and the mattresses. The occupants of the barracks try their hardest to use buckets or pails but it was no use. Diarrhoea was rife throughout the camp: no one enjoyed this foul mess falling upon their head from the bunk above where three people shared a common misery. It was hard to get the energy to wash, in particular on a cold morning, let alone stomach the stench which existed throughout the entire camp, but they would continue to do their best in order to stay alive. But harder than getting dressed was shoving food down your throat in order to attain the energy required to work... it was impossible and so many dropped from exhaustion and were then punished for not doing their work.

The kitchen corporal was seldom late and arrived along with the work details, and already there were men inside lighting the fires for the huge kettles in which to make the watery soup; this was done prior to the smaller kettles being filled and distributed. The kettles in many cases were now ported around on revamped prams, babies and young children being evicted, their bed confiscated for the good of the workers. So it was now that even the men were thinking of their energy and didn't give a damn about the comforts of the so-very young. But strife once again had to be dealt with as over time, one after another, the prams became broken and were cast aside upon a scrap heap beside the dead.

Large hoses were pulled around with two or three women to each, struggling with the anacondas of the kitchen in order to clean out and scrub the kettles of the contents from the night before, which smelt foul but they couldn't tell the difference: what was the difference between the smell of shit and that of the kettles? The smell of the kettles was scrubbed out, but the smell of shit lingers in their nostrils for ever and a day. But they were used to it now – how insane was that, to be used to the smell of shit as though it was smeared upon your upper lip on a hot summer's day?

A single SS guard could be seen half asleep, his hand supporting his head as he gains a few more hours of slumber before being relieved later on in the morning. He could wake at any time, to look around the kitchen to ensure that all were working. These SS were like vipers that wake from a dream and spit venom without second thought, easily triggered into using a whip to thrash at the back of a young woman.

The female inmates were so ugly now that the SS guards rarely looked at them as sexual objects and their fantasies go unfulfilled, and in place of the sexual pleasure came a string of violence and hatred, hatred that was always present but not always released, for some men of the SS were as cunning as dogs, even if out-ranked by them. Any number of inmates would kick a dog but not waste the effort on a thick-headed guard, although one would give a guard a glass of water if he were drowning.

The coffee in the kettles was ready and the kettles lined up for distribution amongst the different huts, and the men come and go as they shuffle away with their heavy loads, putting kettles upon their transports.

It was now time for the kitchen hands to have breakfast; and where the authority of the kitchen was in anything but a very bad temper, then sweet porridge and coffee was consumed in a delectable manner.

By 6:30 the kitchen kettle-washers were joined by many others and the task of washing and cutting vegetables began once more. The wooden benches once sat upon by inmates no longer existed, as they have been used in building other barracks for the influx of poor bastards and bitches that continue to march through the front gates of hell, and so the workers would stand all day and do their duty, getting ready the midday meal of crap which could be poured through a sieve, and if an inmate was lucky then they might find a piece of the vegetable which, having been slaved over all morning to procure from the whole, had found its way into one's mouth.

The meal was cooked in large vats, dozens of them lined up in rows, like the SS. Everything reminded the inmates of the SS; they couldn't get those nasty creatures out of their minds, not for a second.

The men appeared again and moved off with the food containers, delivering the meal to the huts, but no sooner had they gone then they seemed to be back again. Once more the task of cleaning the kettles from the morning coffee begins and ends, and afternoon coffee is prepared, and along with this mammoth task they also have to clean the vats; it was endless, the work just kept on coming.

More food was now prepared for the last meal of the day, which amounts to nothing in real terms and the food was getting less and less, the portions smaller and smaller. At the current rate the food would stop completely and then they would all die, and so, even though the work was hard in the kitchen there was a little reward in the food that was consumed, but the hunger was always present and brave women dared to steal what they could in order to provide husbands with a little something to help them with the hard labour they had to endure.

The night was upon them all and it was time to go back to the barracks. Three women were caught trying to smuggle peel from the grounds and they were summarily punished by being thrown into the bunker.

Whether or not the 'dog woman' paid a visit was mostly up to the guard on duty and the severity of the crime which had been committed.

CHAPTER 24

It was almost morning and the camp was stirring. A woman in a bunk opposite Franzi coughed constantly and yet another scratched uncontrollably from the tier above; it's a dreadful noise. There was a dead body lying next to her and from above there lay another with severe diarrhoea, and the shit fell through the thin mattress and onto Franzi's body of skin over bone, it's warm... a small relief. She could hardly move but had to get out of the hut. She had to wash and get rid of the dead body, but she could hardly move.

It was almost time for roll call and she found it in herself to somehow get to her feet and as she did she looked out upon the ever growing mounting of dead men and women; the SS pride and joy, the world's disgrace and shame.

A figure of a man could be seen staggering towards the mountain of dead, at a height of five to six bodies, and then he collapsed momentarily, nothing more than a stick figure which was hard to see, for the bare flesh of the dead acts as a camouflage for the naked body of the man who finds it hard to stagger into place. But finally he arrived and he crawled into position, a hiding place from which the SS would not find him. He looked as though he was one of the dead, indistinguishable from the other remains. Franzi felt pity for the man, a great surge of sadness falling upon her as she watched, as the man intended to hide from the SS and the roll call, for he obviously didn't have the energy to continue with the work that's forced upon him, and to be forced into work would be the death of him. But there was also sadness for the unnecessary waste, for the man would undoubtedly die where he lay if he stayed there too long. Perhaps it was best; perhaps this was the best thing for him. His sunken eyes closed and he remained still, hoping to crawl out of the mountain of dead later that day, perhaps in time for something to eat and if not... then that would be the last anyone saw of him. He was just one more body to be added to the masses of the dead.

And now the man was forgotten because the SS commenced to call for the parade which was nothing other than a sadistic measure of abuse to add to the war crimes committed by these heinous scum.

Sleep the night before was almost non-existent because the lice saw to it that everyone with the energy to do so spent hour upon hour scratching away at the body until it was so sore that infection sets in and matters of medical concern grow out of control. There was no salvation, no way in which to receive relief. Too tired they all are, all so very tired. But it was not just the lice, but the bedbugs and the fleas, an impossibility to imagine, the suffering that had to be contented with on a day to day basis, where the nights drag on and grow in length: and some think that it is better to suffer the abuse and work by day, receiving beatings upon the head, shoulders and body. It was better to suffer humiliation and insults than suffer another night in the bunks.

The bunks are tiny; barely room enough to sit up on the lower bunks and only just enough space to crawl in and out of your infested space on the upper, each level shared by two to three people. The overcrowding was impossible; and there was no energy to cry, and a cold breeze would often be felt coming through the bare rafters of the roof, to be suffered by those on the top bunk. Which was worse: to suffer a breeze or to be shat upon from the bunk above? It was a question without an answer for both meant the same thing in the end; an unpleasant death.

The passage down the centre of the barrack was impossible to negotiate. There was shit all over the floor from the diarrhoea, and the stench was growing worse and worse: the Jews knew this as a fact because they had become so accustomed to the stink of the whole damn place that for it to smell worse than the day before would surely mean a further slump in hygiene: such a stupid word to use; hygiene. It simply didn't exist; nowhere except possibly in the SS quarters, their clothing store, or the doctor's office – oh, and not to forget that saint of a man, Joseph Kramer, who was so loving that his relationship with Irma Grese was more than lust, for although it was a relatively clandestine arrangement between them, where love making was as pathetic as their claims to be human, the torture of the prisoners was talked about over meals, and their intentions, to be drawn upon the weak on the morrow, were shared with smiles upon their faces.

Irma Grese passionately stroked Kramer's scar and kissed it. Such was life to be a whore and the devil. To speak their names seemed a crime in itself and so often it was heard amongst the Jews that the Criminal did this, or the Dog Woman did that, but Irma Grese was not to be confused with Juana Bormann who was known quite categorically as 'the woman with the dogs'. Such wretched people didn't deserve an ounce of recognition, no more than Hitler, deserving to be denied the opportunity to be recognized as a man of history, for he was nothing more than a murdering bastard.

To Franzi it seemed plain and simple: Kramer was the master, and she was the dog, and the allies were the animal lovers coming to her rescue. Yes; she was falling insane, the torment of time in this place being too hard to overcome.

CHAPTER 25

The men and women of the camp moved around half naked in most cases, in particular when in the washrooms. There was no embarrassment and everyone looked the same, for the women, in general, no longer had breasts, and there was not an ounce of interest in the opposite sex for the sake of recreational or horizontal pleasure. Such luxuries of human existence had disappeared a long time ago. Each sex moved around as though oblivious to the other, where each person was nothing more than a skeleton wrapped up in tight skin.

Franzi no longer bothered to avert her eyes; no one else did; it's not even a contemplation of mind: no one cared anymore.

And the morning's ablutions were finished with, but stomachs still turned over and shit fell freely to the floor.

Roll call was made and there were people missing, either too sick or too exhausted to come out into the open, but the open was better than being cooped up in a hut full of faeces, lice and lingering disease.

Franzi looked up and down the mass of Jews lined up for roll call and noticed that there were already close to a hundred skeletons – known as people – standing up and facing the fence, being punished for some damned unknown and ludicrous reason for which the SS guards had decided to punish. It was beyond foolishness. But the guards made up excuses, be it laziness, late for roll call, late for work, answering back, speaking without permission, not standing up straight, being too ugly, looking a guard in the eye... it didn't matter for a reason could be found and it was easy for the SS to find a reason for they had been doing it for so long that it now came natural. It was second nature for a guard to issue a punishment, giving a reason why such was being placed upon the individual, and all carried out without the guard so much as looking upon the person being punished.

A SS guard entered a barrack building with the kapo, Kasimir Cegielski, and found the culprits, five men and three women.

Nigel B.J.Clayton

They were accused of being lazy. They were a 'bunch of lazy pigs' according to the SS and extremely unlucky in the eyes of those at roll call. Franzi only wished, with all the strength she had left within her fragile body, that they wouldn't be punished so severely, but the SS made everyone stand for so long at roll call when they could have been sitting down in the kitchen and trying to put peel into their mouths.

The SS were mostly young men; fit and strong, healthy, well fed and muscular; but all they did was abuse, and beat, and beat some more. And so there were beatings to follow and more punishment after that.

They were beaten, all eight of them, beaten excessively and ordered over to the fence; there they were made to stand all day.

A guard offered some advice on how he had to remain standing for hours on end, doing his duty, and the lazy Jews got to sit down and rip apart a few pairs of shoes, or the men of the 'tree commando' got to work in the open, away from the filth. His complaints go on death ears, but the guard believed in what he said and abused those at roll call by making them stand for two hours without a move: move and you get whipped, fall down and you get whipped some more; fail to stand up when whipped and its bunker.

Finally Franzi got her opportunity to attend the kitchen and she managed to do her work and get some peel into her mouth, and by the day's end she fell out of the kitchen along with the others she had endured her day with. Then she saw those at the fence.

The eight men and women sent to the fence remained there until well after the sun had gone down, after which they would be permitted back into the barracks: after being issued the disgruntled whipping from guards to hurry them along.

There was no justice; Franzi couldn't take much more. She walked towards the women on the fence, to give them an encouraging word. A guard saw her stray from the move back to the barracks and Franzi was absconded to the bunker for three days without bread or water.

94

One of the women had fallen dead and two men and one woman taken for further punishment to the bunker below ground. A further two men, found to have potatoes in their possession the day before, stolen from the SS storehouse, were summarily sentenced to 28 days bunker, where they were secretly taken away and fed to the dogs.

CHAPTER 26

The inmates numbered over 15,000 in late December 1944, and now, in late March, there were in excess of 44,000 of them; it was ridiculous; it was simply beyond all contemplation.

The labourers for the chopping of wood were gathered and marched away and on reaching their destination were fallen out to commence the arduous task they had been so unfairly targeted with, but not before two men were pulled aside for talking out of place. They were summarily punished by being forced to stand bent over with their hands open and palms upon the ground. They remained in this position for an hour.

A man asked whether or not they'd be able to stand upright by themselves after the punishment was over with and the comment didn't go unpunished – he was beaten to death in front of everyone.

That evening the men returned and got their ration, which consisted of what would be barely enough to feed a two-year old child. How the men worked on such small portions, without any measure of nutrition within, was beyond contemplation.

On return a man fell slovenly over his own feet and tripped another two behind him. He was extracted from the commando as it came to a halt and made to stand for four hours in front of the fence as punishment for bringing condemnation upon the parade. He was later returned to his barracks with a flogging to the back of the head to drink his soup of spinach water which his wife had managed to barter for, swapping her diamond wedding ring - extracted from orifice - in order that her husband could have something before retiring to bed. The pity in her eyes was enough to make anyone cry and wince in pain.

But the following morning seemed to bring a little sunshine and a group of thirty-five prisoners were drafted together with an excursion to come. They were to be escorted into the forest where it had been discovered that wild potatoes were growing in abundance. The men were to be put to work with digging up the potable food and to also see how extensive the commodity was.

The men were given their orders and several sacks in which to bring back what they found. They stood as erect as they possibly could and nearly all of them were smiling, for they were going on a walk into the wilderness, away from the camp, to bring something back for them and their families – where families existed.

The gates in front of them opened and then closed again as they passed through, and the sergeant of the work party ordered them left and right and left again until they were ordered to halt.

The walk had been marvellous and the fresh air was beyond belief; it was so different out here away from the camp, away from the stench... away from the security of the wire fence, and it was then that the guards unshoulder their weapons and shot dead all thirty-five of the prisoners.

There were no potatoes there in the forest.

The guards returned to camp and the sergeant reported that there had been an attempted breakout; that the prisoners did try to escape. His duty was done; he will sleep well tonight; he was proud to be a German.

CHAPTER 27

There was a little commotion, something out of the ordinary was occurring. A POW from an adjoining camp was being extricated from his surroundings and brought along the main road towards Josef Kramer's office, though the devil himself was waiting for the arrival of the prisoner from outside one of the barrack huts, where the mounting dead were in easy view.

The gentleman walked with pride, the crisp air on this 28th day of March being felt upon his face, his head held high; he was a soldier of the British Royal Marines.

The marine's guard of two were nothing more than an escort as the British soldier walked along between them, neither offering resistance of any description nor allowing himself to be tormented by the smell and horror of so many dead. He knew what the camp was like; he'd not been far from it for some time now, and the smell always drifted across into his section of the camp.

The marine came to a stop in front of the commandant and looked him in the eye, seeing the devilish mind tick over as it waited for a salute, a salute which was never going to come.

Some time passed before Kramer opened his mouth. "I've heard of your insolence," said Kramer, "and of your failure to help us with questions that we have surrounding a certain... shall I say... conspiracy."

"This is war, Hauptsurmführer," announced the marine, "I fail to see where conspiracy fits into it."

"Ah, at least you've remembered me; a pity you can't remember to salute."

"I know why I'm here, more or less, and you'll find that I shall continue to... disappoint you. I've told all of those that have interrogated me that I know nothing."

"Of course you don't, that's why we're going to... have a quiet word," said Kramer. "This way, please."

The small congregation continued on towards the bunker but stopped just short as the door burst open.

Franzi was being escorted out by the scuff of the neck, battered well from behind as she fell through the open door and into relative freedom. She was happy to see the sky again, happy to have lived through punishment known as the bunker.

Kramer looked stifled by the upset of the composure of the prisoner and of the guards as they did their best to keep within arm's reach of the one under their care and beat her with their truncheons once more.

"You stupid, shit-whore!" shouted one of the guards. It was then that he noticed Kramer and immediately came to attention and paid his compliments.

"Carry on," said Kramer and turned to see one of the marine's escorts being brushed aside by the Brit, by a forceful hand, as the guard endeavoured to usher the British soldier through the open door.

Franzi fell to the ground again and looked around and up to the marine standing there, so peaceful and serene he seemed to be, with marks upon his face where he'd obviously been beaten.

"Ah!" yelled Kramer. "Trying to escape," he accused.

"I don't take kindly to being man-handled," said the marine as he looked one of the guards in the face.

"Do you intend to answer my questions?" forced Kramer.

"I have nothing to say," said the marine.

"Shoot this man," directed Kramer to one of the guards.

"Sir?" stated the stunned guard.

"Shoot this damn man; he's trying to escape... now!"

The guard pulled his revolver from its hiding and pointed it at the head of the marine who did nothing other than smile. The weapon was fired and the body fell to the ground.

"Get his clothes off and hide his body amongst those other vermin; for he's no better than a stinking Jew," directed Kramer and stepped off briskly to his office.

"Get on your feet, you slut!" yelled the guard from the bunker, pulling Franzi up by the roots of her hair. "On your feet bitch before I give you cause to lie down again."

Franzi was stunned beyond belief. The marine had just been

killed in cold blood. Wasn't it enough that they, the innocent, should be treated so badly, to be indiscriminately killed for no other reason than to appease the frantic madness of Hitler; but to kill a soldier in such a way, without good cause, was beyond the code of conduct of men at war?

CHAPTER 28

The SS guard, Gertrude Sauer, stood at arm's length from the prisoner to her front and stepped back a little, the smell from the Polish woman's armpit most terrible, a smell which was slapping the guard in the face: the sight of the lice crawling over her skin almost making her sick.

"Get it up; higher!" yelled Gertrude.

Piroska could say nothing, had no option but to do as she was ordered. The strain upon her was enormous. She was being punished for stealing a pumpkin, punished on the first day of April as though she was some joke.

Further noises of strain came from deep within the Polish prisoner, grunting in her effort to keep the pumpkin above her head and at arm's length.

"You stinking, whore-thief. Stoning is too good for you Polish bitches," yelled Gertrude as she walked around Piroska's front, hitting her own palm with the whip she carried, drawing the Jew's eyes to the instrument of her fear. She had been beaten too often these past few days and for no other reason than being a Polish Jew.

"Keep that pumpkin up if you want to live," warned Gertrude. She came around the back of Piroska and lashed out with a hit to the back of her legs, which were by now quite red and burning with pain.

Piroska almost dropped the pumpkin but managed to keep control of it. It's amazing how heavy a pumpkin got, how small it first appeared.

"Did you sleep with many guards in Auschwitz?" demanded Gertrude of her plaything. She struck again the back of the legs, harder than before and the pumpkin came down to Piroska's waist before quickly being lifted again above her head. Again the stinging of Gertrude's whip hits her on the back of the legs.

"Drop it again and its bunker for you," warns Gertrude who was beginning to grow tired of the game she played. She had better things to do, a meal to eat and fresh water to drink; a slice of bread and cheese perhaps: she also knew a woman companion who had some chocolate of which she could share.

Piroska grunted again, her continuing effort to keep the pumpkin above her head drawing every ounce of energy that she had, but her punishment was almost over for Gertrude was hungry.

Piroska wasn't sure how she could continue at this pace, holding the pumpkin up above her head, but she knew it meant her survival so she would do all she could. The pains in her body would have to be forgotten, the pain in her arms and legs brushed aside; she would have to rise above this torture so that she could experience free life once more, to endure a free life filled with bad memories.

Gertrude stopped in front of her prisoner. "Put the pumpkin down." Piroska obeyed with much relief, and then came the final blow. Gertrude lashed out with one almighty whipping to Piroska's face, knocking the Polish woman to the ground.

Several teeth were knocked loose and there was now a small cut above her lip where bruising was quick to form.

"Get up on your feet, you stupid bitch, before I find a red-hot poker to shove up your arse," threatened Gertrude. "Now take that pumpkin to the kitchen, where it belongs, and if I see you thieving again then it will be the death penalty for you."

And so Piroska picked up the pumpkin with her face bleeding and did what she had to do before seeking rest in her hut.

CHAPTER 29

It was a reasonably pleasant Sunday and a small congregation of inmates looked out towards the main gate of their camp. There was a truck and it was destined for the kitchen.

What a relief such a sight was and everyone knew where it was destined for. No other reason existed for a truck to be brought into the confines of their misery unless it was to deliver food of some description – maybe it was something other than turnip.

The truck drove along and the driver, being either ignorant or simply without the skills to drive the vehicle, ran over a body lying upon the ground.

A bag of raw turnips was loosely sealed within the back and several pieces fell from the truck and onto the ground, a half dozen or more; they were rotten and squashed easily as they hit the hard surface of the ground, but some survived the fall.

Corporal Otto Calesson saw the look in the eyes of the prisoners and called to the guard nearby to look at what was about to unfold.

"Anchor, you will see what happens when scum are hungry," said Otto before calling out to those watching for any sign of a guard's presence. "You prisoners; you can help yourself to what lies on the road."

The inmates suddenly burst into a run – a fast walk by normal standards – to try and be the first upon the scattered vegetables. They pushed and shoved and fought their way forward. The SS guards laughed and simply couldn't believe the sight they saw before them.

"Do you know what's so funny?" asked Otto of his companion, a new guard having just arrived from training.
"Other than the fact that they look like hungry dogs after a feast, they resemble skeletons fighting for a fur coat," answered Anchor.

"Yes... yes... that is so true," and Otto laughed some more along with Anchor. "But those turnips; they are destined for

Kramer's personal pen of twenty-five pigs. It is rotten turnip, not good for the kitchen... no good for human consumption."

"Then it's good that these scum aren't human," said a sergeant from behind.

Otto turned to see the sergeant smiling.

"I see you have found yourselves something attractive to keep you busy," said the sergeant.

"I was just introducing my friend to the prisoners," said Otto in defence.

"I'm not scolding you, dear Otto," said the sergeant. "But next time you plan a party like this, make sure to let me know. There's nothing more I like than to watch a show where the scum of the earth fight so hard for something destined for the trough of a pig," and commenced laughing himself.

And the inmates continued to squabble as they fought over the rotten turnips, drawing what they could into their mouths, regardless of the taste. Those that were hungry for a mouthful of something... anything... it didn't matter what it tasted like, so long as it filled the emptiness of the stomach; even if temporarily. Even a piece of dried up leather would be better than nothing.

Oscar, one of the inmates, missed out on the turnips. He received a knock in the head and a kick in the thigh, and yet he received nothing. He was too slow, too exhausted, and too damn hungry.

He fell back from the ravenous dogs scrambling on the ground, eating what they could salvage from the rotten turnips, and saw the three guards turn their backs on them before retiring.

Oscar fell to the ground from the sheer exhaustion of it all. He had been mentally scarred by all that had gone on around him. For so long he had been here in this camp of pestilence; so long in fact that he could not remember anything else of the world before Bergen-Belsen. This camp was his entire life; of what he could recall of it.

He finally managed to get onto his hands and knees and with

much effort commenced to crawl towards a shiny object on the ground near the mountain of dead. He drew closer to it, bit by bit, and soon realised that it was a small knife used for eating. It's been so long since he's used a knife that he's not sure if he knows how. He's used to drinking soup from a bowl and shoving bread in his mouth, but not eating with a knife.

He finally got within distance and reached out, grabbing it by its handle. It drew it near and looked at it, and from his peripheral he saw a dead body lying on the ground next to the mountain of rotting flesh. The body was reasonably new. The man he saw would have died just that morning, or even later than that. It was even possible that his heart was still warm... lovely and tender... succulent and rewarding.

He moved up to the dead body and fell across it and with great precision he cut into the chest of the dead, cutting as best he could a hole to the heart. He managed, after several minutes, to extricate himself several mouthfuls of heart and he put it into his mouth. He started to chew. Mmmm; so lovely it was; real meat. It's like heaven to him, like nothing before he's tasted these past few years. It's better than a juicy steak, better than sausage, or pie, or ham off the bone. He couldn't believe how good it was, how lucky he was to get to it first. He no longer cared about the damn turnips for he had found something much better and far more rewarding.

He sinks his teeth again and again into the muscle of the heart and was momentarily satisfied for the meal, when, with a sudden surge of normality, his mind cleared way to clear thinking and he realised what had become of him.

He wept silently to himself for what he had done; for what could not be undone, and he could not be forgiven. He had eaten man-flesh, he had sinned a terrible sin. He had molested another human being, defiled what should not be defiled. He could never forgive himself for what he had done.

CHAPTER 30

Ernst Kaltenbrunner was the head of the Reich Security Main Office and it came into his palm, a direct order from Hitler himself, that all of the prisoners of Bergen-Belsen were to be summarily killed as it wasn't fitting that the prisoners should be allowed to fall into the hands of the Allies, not alive in any case. He then passed this order on to Kramer who received it with as little emotion that could possibly be evoked from such an order. To Kramer the death of thousands meant little to him, for if he'd really cared then he would have done something long before now.

But it came to pass that negotiations with the British were about to commence in regards to Bergen-Belsen, negotiations which very well might see to it that war crimes against humanity might be diverted if it could be seen that the fault of the killings was derived from actions compounded by certain figures of the Third Reich, or even individual members of the SS itself. Kramer would do well to receive such a favourable outlook in the circumstances that war had dealt him. Not only this, but a kind word from Felix Kersten, a Swedish chiropractor that had treated Himmler, saw to it that the order was reversed and Kramer handed the opportunity of a lifetime; Himmler had now taken control of the dying situation to try and save a little face, and Kramer, too, saw his opportunity.

Himmler felt the distaste of imprisonment in his mouth. It was the first week of April and he knew, as others did too, that the war would soon be over. Although he had never really changed his tune in regards to the treatment of the prisoners, and naive in regards to the way in which they were treated, needed to now ensure that some form of action was carried out in order to save his own neck. He'd originally ordered the Head of the Gestapo, Heinrich Müller, to keep the prisoners healthy and alive, this ordered back in 1943; and now he faced the implication of being partly responsible for the Jews disposition: and so he was.

Josef Kramer, the Camp's Commandant, was the man with

two faces: one of evil and the other a mask that portrayed a kind-hearted individual: but nothing could be further from the truth. The scale of the genocide present within his camp was simply unforgiving and orchestrated well by him and the SS. But now, something had to be done to make it look as though Kramer had made an effort to aid these poor creatures of the community. Along with Dr Fritz Cline, his chief physician, the camp was quarantined and an order for the transport of vegetables and meat was handed out to the appropriate authorities that he had in his reach. But it was to no avail and his struggle to see him placed out of harm's way had no effect upon his disposition, his past lack of human decency overshadowing his meagre attempts.

Himmler, also, needed to act quickly if he was to extricate himself from accusations which he could see were forthcoming and so over the next five days saw to it that an order of his was executed without question. Three transports of prisoners from within the camp of Bergen-Belsen were to be evacuated, more if possible. The order saw to it that Kramer acted with a little jest in his step for the first time in many years and prisoners from the Neutral camp, the Star Camp, and the Hungarian Camp, were evacuated under consideration that they were 'exchange Jews' and held foreign passports.

Surely, Himmler thought, a little justice would go a long way and with such actions of charity would come some forgiveness; and he needed the allies on his side, secretly wishing for the allies to join with Germany in a war against Russia.

CHAPTER 31

The water ration was stopped, no more soup; and no more bread, nothing at all to come the prisoners' way. Everything had stopped on 7th April, as though a cork in a bottle had been rammed tight. There was no water supply whatsoever to speak of. This was a catastrophe beyond all others. The unhealthy and the sick, which comprised everyone within the camp, were absolutely reliant on water and simply couldn't live without it.

The Germans were losing the war, a great loss to their precious Third Reich and its abilities to perform. If they were to lose then the Jews should lose too.

The amount of spite that the Germans felt for these poorly treated Jews was so insurmountable that it simply could not be registered. The feelings of the SS towards these people were just so understated that it was impossible to contemplate that such hatred could exist. What did the Jew do that was so damaging to the German way of life? Many of them owned businesses of all description and led a clean way of life, never pestering others nor bludging off of the government in any way or form; why should they be dealt such a bad card in life?

And so the SS seldom entered the camps from this day on and roll calls, although continuing, were not as frequent, allowing the sick to die in relative peace: if struggling with insurmountable pain could be considered as being 'peaceful'.

Work parties were seen to drop almost immediately but some work needed to be maintained, such as the forced labour suffered when being handed the duty to unblock the sewerage, returning to the barracks covered in vile filth, shit and piss.

And so the days continued, individuals doing all they could to see that they survived the war, but there was still no end in sight, regardless of the air raids and planes overhead. The misery of the entire situation was growing by the hour, getting worse and worse by the day. There seemed to be no relief to come and many felt that the coming days would see them die, just as their friends had died before them, or family members had been given a farewell as they were carted away to be burnt at the crematorium or thrown upon the mountain of dead like common garbage. It seemed to many of them that that's what they had become; common garbage to be brushed aside, to decay in the gutters of society.

Was there not a single person in the world that cared about them?

CHAPTER 32

On April 8th, around 30,000 more prisoners were injected into the camp of Bergen-Belsen, an unbelievable number to say the least. No food, no water, and more prisoners. Here was a camp built for no more than 10,000 and in the matter of hours it had swelled out of all proportion.

For those of the camp that could get to a window, or even a door, the sight of all the people entering the camp under the whippings of the guards was simply too much to bear and so these wretched thousands, the newcomers to hell, had backs turned upon them.

There was little hope for survival now, little hope to see the war through. Conditions within the camp were bad enough as it was, but now; it was sheer torture of the likes no one had seen since the age of chivalry.

From all over the Neuengamme area they came, all of the camps within that geographic location evacuated and placed in the hands of Kramer and his whip-wielding guards. The camp now numbered over 60,000 prisoners from all sectors of life, from prisoners of war to civilian Jews; there was no quarter of the community at large that was exempt from Hitler's insanity or his call for the continuing murder of innocents, and so the torture and atrocities went on.

So many prisoners and so few places left to house them.

The dilapidated barracks were full with three-tiered bunks and the stables full to the brim, and tents were used to the extreme of insanity. But one call for clemency was heard, one call and one call only, from the pages of the Geneva Convention.

The typhus epidemic, along with the guidelines as laid down by the Geneva Convention, was considered well, and it also suited the Nazis for whom wished to maintain a cruel hold of the Jews of their camps. It was not possible to evacuate diseased prisoners and so the overflow was cramped ever more into accommodation already bursting at the seams: yes indeed, the Nazis made something of this rule.

Down the road, the Army Training Centre was also used for its asset, the barracks adjacent and in close enough proximity to the severity of guards under Kramer, for them to continue with their cruelty. Fifteen thousand prisoners were transferred here.

CHAPTER 33

There were so many bodies lying around that it was an unbelievable sight, even to those closest to the circumstances so rife. Thousands upon thousands were lying in small mountains, some having decayed a lot and others just starting to smell of that sickly odour known as death. And so the SS, under the orders of Kramer, made what was seen as their final effort to hold back the tide of accusations against them by burying bodies in mass graves in remote spots away from the camp, where it was hoped that the allies would not find them. On this day, April 11th, commenced the hiding of the dead.

Another mass grave was being dug nearer the barracks but wasn't as large as the other. It appeared as though the SS were trying to outwit the British by consecrating a few bodies in graves under their noses but concealing the majority far away and out of sight. It was the threat of war crimes which lingered in the air. The work was also continued during the night, aided by the light given off by kerosene lamps. Work parties were now mostly organised to dig and bury, not to peel and cook.

As the SS worked, their white armbands slipped from their upper arms, little flags of truce which showed their concerns for the advancing allies; this was their sign of surrender: but the atrocities continued behind their masquerade. It was a true account of their courage and bravery, where they pretended to display their cooperation and willingness to cease with hostilities but continued with the atrocities which were fixed like pillars of iron within their heads. It was said many times that you should never accept a gift from a Greek; maybe it will now be understood, for all time, that you should never accept the cooperation, leniency, or assurance of a Nazi, regardless of the form in which they showed themselves; past, present, or future; because as with the gift from Greece, the after-affect was always death.

For three days, until the 14th, all available prisoners, regardless of age, who were in condition to be forced to work, were pulled into line and made to bury the dead. It was a struggle against the clock, a means by which to avoid the accusations of war crimes.

Kramer, the 'Beast of Belsen', permitted the use of music to spur the work on and as over 2,000 men and women dragged the remains of human life along the ground, two orchestras played music under the guidance of the guards.

The dead were dragged around with the aid of leashes, straps of leather or cloth attached to wrists and ankles. From the time the sun appeared on the horizon and until it disappeared from view at night the inmates were forced to work their fingers to the bone, shifting thousands upon thousands of bodies from the camp and into mass graves. Whoever said you couldn't move mountains, for several piles of human monstrosity, of deathly carnage, were moved over the dreadful period of four days but still, even after so much work and effort, there were still over 10,000 corpses that remained in place.

The guards were at their least merciful now, for they were seeing to it that they survived the war. The guards wished to see their families again, to see their mothers and fathers; none cared for the Jew. It was nothing to a Nazi that the wretches under their guard should fall by the way and succumb to the calling of their brethren who lay dead and without voice amongst the 10,000 in view.

The whips of the guards rained heaviest now, more than ever before. The use of their bayonets drew more blood in the few days of burial than they'd seen all year. The SS had been given a true gift, for it didn't matter if a prisoner died now as they could simply be thrown into the grave in which was being filled. So a man was clubbed over the head and fell unconscious to the unhallowed ground; so what? He was still breathing and had the taste of life on his tongue, could smell the air around him – and although it stinks of foulness it was still pertinent to life. The guards ordered the Jews close at hand to continue with the filling of the mass grave, the earth covering over the recently fallen. Men and women were buried alive, rubbed from existence as though a bad stain in life.

    The SS guards didn't give a damn and the flag of truce upon their sleeves meant nothing to them except that it was a piece of cloth in which to wipe their sweaty brow, sweat from the hard labour of flogging the sick.

CHAPTER 34

As the sun reached its highest point in the sky on April 12th, a Mercedes carrying a white flag upon its bonnet appeared out of nowhere, two German colonels pulling up in front of the British 159th Battalion's forward headquarters.

The entourage stepped out of the vehicle in the style of a true gentleman, but these officers were Nazis too, and couldn't be counted on, for their camouflage of humbleness hid their true maliciousness and their well-spoken sentences of choreographed speech were flawed with their efforts in trying to receive reprieve for those under their command.

Stepping out in front of their hosts the Germans were greeted in the usual fashion that one would expect. This was Colonel Schmidt and Lieutenant Colonel Bohnekamp; with them were a medical officer and a translator.

The two German officers presented themselves in their full regalia, stone-cold and hard faces looking from below the rim of their peaked caps, their uniforms an example of how an officer should be dressed – it was the task of the lackey to perform the daily maintenance upon an officers kit and make coffee on demand: it was usually obvious as to how many slaves a single commander had under his sway by the way in which he dressed and carried himself.

The two German officers were then blindfolded and taken to 8 Corps Headquarters where negotiations were to be drawn up between the two forces; negotiations which the Germans hoped would bring about a toned reception in reflection of their kindness.

There was an exhausting underestimation on behalf of the German pigs who tried to deal the hand they held as best as possible, indicating with a rather cool and collective, very straight face, that there were 9,000 sick in the camp of Bergen-Belsen, when in fact the number was so much higher, and many had typhus. The British officers were alarmed by such a number, and had it been revealed of the true scale and nature of the situation regarding the matter then the German officers may have been shackled right then and there.

"We have a request which might sound... surprising," said the German to the British officer to his front, "but in the interests of the Geneva Convention, and for the preservation of life, we are indebted to advise you of a problem which has come about from the allied bombings of the rail network and roads in the vicinity of this camp."

"Please continue," said the British officer.

"Supplies to the camp have been cut off around the towns of Bergen and Belsen. In this vicinity is a camp which houses approximately fifty-thousand prisoners, nine thousand of which are sick, some with typhus; there is no available water, no medical supplies and very little food. Each time we try to supply the camp your aircraft destroys the supplies. We currently have over two-thousand Hungarian and German regular soldiers guarding the camp."

"And SS?"

"Yes; of course," admitted the German. "There are SS, too, but most are administrational staff, which is a different matter altogether," and the fake within his voice betrayed the German officer. "I am happy to arrange for them to help you with the transition of the camp."

"I see," answered the British officer.

"We wish you to occupy the camp as soon as possible," said the German, hurriedly, avoiding further talk of the SS, "in order to prevent any outbreak of disease in accordance with international interests of health and safety." It was a remarkable feat in itself that the officer could keep a straight face whilst laying his cards upon the table. "We wish to offer a limited truce."

"That's absurd. We already have a bridgehead over the river Aller and have crossed over this with our tanks, as you well know. You'll have to offer more than a simple truce." said the British officer, General Taylor-Balfour, still startled by the fact that 9,000 inmates were sick; he was disgusted. He could feel his stomach turn over with the thought of so many helpless people: trapped and helpless they were. "The truce is in your favour, not ours. Our advance upon your lines and safe havens give us the overwhelming advantage. Taking care of this camp, Bergen-Belsen, will only impede us more."

The officer was silent for a moment. "We can offer to you and your forces another bridge over the river Aller and we will also propose not to destroy this."

The British thought then: how desperate these Nazis were.

The German officers knew that the death rate in the camp was growing by the day and that, even as they spoke, the dead were being buried in secret locations to hide the atrocities. There was a fine point in allowing the British an early entry to the camp, but it was also a bad decision to allow the situation to worsen by postponing any action against the outbreak of disease; after all, this was still Germany and the lives of civilians were at stake.

"We must have complete control of the area around the camp, for at least six kilometres all around. We must be permitted to keep our lines of communication open at all costs, and your petty offerings don't allow us to continue with the advance as we would like. We can commit to the aid and the taking over of the camp, for the good of the community at large, but must have a clearer understanding as to ownership and control in order to prevent any of the sick from spreading disease."

The German officers were frantic at the thought of 'ownership' but had nowhere else to turn. "We will give you what you have suggested. You can have the bridge and the area immediately around the camp. We would formally request map coordinates in order to see the arrangements met."

"But the typhus is a problem and I can see no alternative but to seal off the area as soon as possible," said the British officer.

"I agree with this," said the German. "It is in all our interests to prevent further tragedy."

"Might I suggest that you mount posts at either end of the area to warn of the typhus epidemic; you can man these with unarmed guards."

"Unarmed?" asked the German.

"We cannot have armed Germans in an area deemed to be under British control; not unless you, an officer, intends to stand at the post yourself, or the intervening commander of our forces permits the carriage of such weapons," and the sparkle in the British officer's eyes saw the German submit to defeat. "I'll require your full cooperation. All Germans in the camp are to wear white armbands in order for us to know that they accept these terms, and they are to perform duties as required."

"White armbands; yes, that has already been done."

"You do work quickly, don't you, Colonel?"

"My interest is in saving lives," said the German.

"A German soldier, saving lives," said the British officer curtly.

"I agree to your request for your requirement to fulfil your duties and our responsibilities, but the regular army must be released so that they can continue with their duties to Germany, bearing arms and their equipment. This I must insist upon."

"As you wish," said the British officer. "I'll have my orderly see to it immediately and then we can sign some papers. I'm sure there will be some finer details that need to be considered, but all-in-all I think we can agree on the manner of the predicament. As for the SS guards; one is no different than another. Any personnel that remain behind will be deemed as guards, regardless of uniform, one and all, and subjected to military law. A soldier is a soldier; is he not?"

The German was silent for a second and then nodded in defeat. "Yes, I suppose they are." Their lives now rested on the quick burial of the dead, but he would warn Kramer of the likely predicament that was awaiting the SS guards, for he knew they wouldn't be received well.

"Good," said the British officer. "I'm glad we could come to some agreement on this matter. It's of the greatest importance to prevent an epidemic as early as possible."

The achievement in organizing the limited truce was beyond imagination to many, but for war crimes convictions to be dropped, Bergen-Belsen was to become a power-pawn for the Germans. Negotiations were fierce; more so from the British side of the argument, and in rather a fast committal of past actions the British accepted what it was that the German authorities had to offer. The agreement was for the avoidance of battle in the area surrounding the camp. The agreement saw to it that a neutral zone was established around the camp and was estimated at around 48 square kilometres, being eight in length and six in width.

There was agreement that the British would take over control of the camp, that the German SS and regular army would be replaced by the allies, the towers to take the form of a cordon to contain the disease and general outbreak of typhus as opposed to forming a ring of iron where rifles lashed out their evil from time to time upon the unsuspecting. The British bombing and shelling of the area ceased almost immediately. It was also clearly made understood that most of the SS guards would be removed and their role as guards taken up by Hungarian soldiers and the German regular army prior to the British arriving, if not already carried out, although the SS administration staff, in general, would remain in situ until the British took control of Bergen-Belsen and allowed the SS to retreat back to their duties elsewhere, be it another camp or fighting somewhere near the front line. The assurance of allowing the SS staff, and regular soldiers, safe passage from the campgrounds within six days was not a watertight agreement and allowed for much interpretation. There were reported to be a battalion of German infantry and a Hungarian regiment in situ at the camp, and the Hungarians, although subjected to work under the British, would need to be set free at some stage in the future.

A cease-fire agreement was therefore reached between the British Chief of Staff, General Taylor-Balfour and the German Military Commander of the area around Bergen-Belsen.

CHAPTER 35

An English officer was escorted by two SS guards, on Friday 13th of April, rifles by their side and bayonets fixed. The officer had a white flag.

His curiosity was too much for him and he looked constantly, left and right, looking over the mountains of dead, and unbelievable they were in his view, for he had never seen so many dead in a single place at the same time. Never before in his entire life had he seen such slaughter.

The look upon the faces of the guards could not be more displeasing, the obvious power they once held now evaporated. Their hands had been washed of all supremacy and now they were about to be dealt the vengeance that the inmates so wished they'd have to suffer. They had never suffered defeat in their lives, but their fathers and mothers had known of a time, when Hitler was nothing more than a corporal and running errands for officers, when twenty-seven years earlier they had their arses whipped by those unwilling to be treated by fists of iron.

The prisoners who looked upon the British officer knew almost immediately that he was an ally, although most considered the idea that he was nothing more than another prisoner, a prisoner of war that was going to be subjected to the free will of Josef Kramer and either sent immediately to the bunker or killed.

A few of the inmates were encouraged to see that the man was in fact rather clean and had obviously arrived from a quarter where there was little fighting, or that his role in the army was not that which involved the day to day slaughter of the enemy, where it was one of a soldiers many duties to try and gather as much of the enemies blood upon his bayonet as was humanly possible. No, this officer was a class above the rest, intelligent, and respected by his peers.

When the British officer disappeared out of view the men and women of the camp commenced to talk, even the sores in their mouths unable to stop them from remarking on the appearance of one so clean and orderly: it was nothing compared to the talk that became a story and retold many times that late afternoon and evening, of the officer that went to see Kramer, and then returned by the same way in which he had entered, and without a single mark upon him.

The talk of liberation once more filled the air of some of the huts but remained relatively quiet amongst the camp as a whole. The days spent burying the dead had seen to it that many were too exhausted and traumatised to even contemplate the appearance of a saviour, too victimised to think that the war would soon be over and that they would all be free.

On his return to the British command post the officers had trouble accepting that such atrocity awaited them. How could it be true that so many dead existed in this camp, that the bodies could simply be exposed to the elements of the weather, for diseases to filter out amongst the prisoners of the camp and subject them to all manner of horror and distaste? Surely the visiting officer had seen but a small part of the camp which constituted the bulk of the 9,000 sick inmates having been herded together for some reason, and not the main camp itself, and that the shock of what he saw was an exaggeration. The obvious shock of seeing so many dead and dying within the camp was too much for the officer to bear. As for the mountains of dead described by him, it could only have been an error in judgement on his behalf and the bodies themselves were surely stacked upon mounds of dirt or high ground, not upon other bodies hidden beneath: surely there must have been a plausible reason as to why it stood so high. It seemed ludicrous that such a report should come back to them, in particular when assurances had been given that the camp held but 9,000 sick and 41,000 in assumed good health, and that there was no mention of so many dead. The camp was large indeed, several quarters to the whole, this Jewish quarter by far the worst.

Why would the Germans be so anxious to hand over a camp in such a dilapidated state?

CHAPTER 36

The situation in the camp was suddenly made worse by an episode of Nazi cruelty that simply could not be explained. The sheer audacity of those in one of the towers overlooking a water supply point came to air.

Water for washing was made so scarce that disease was soaring and hygiene was plummeting to an all-new low, a point needing no clarity by those suffering the ordeals being suffered, nor confirmation from the SS guards who orchestrated the conditions now infesting the camp.

The conditions were rife and although acknowledged were not provided any attention whatsoever by the guards, and clean water for drinking was even scarcer, much worse now than ever before. It was one thing to make water soup from filthy water, but to put the same repugnant water into your mouth in order to quench the thirst that hung there was a deplorable state of affairs: and watery soup was now but a dream of many for it was no longer being served.

Water was a commodity taken for granted so often, a substance of life and great worth; it was relatively easy to obtain – considering the topography and geographic location of Bergen-Belsen – but it was denied the thousands that relied upon it the most as they continued to decay with the rest of the camp, becoming buried under a mountain of human faeces. But the guards drank well and the dogs drank too, for the guards loved their dogs as much as the dogs loved their sport of ripping flesh from faces. But there was a pump not so far away from several of the barracks, a pump that could give them all the water they needed.

The eyes of the imprisoned darted this way and that, sizing up the opposition; sizing up their cruelty and the lengths to which they would go to in order to bring punishment upon them all.

The Jews knew well that the SS were mostly vacant the towers aloft, and that Hungarian guards had taken their places. What had a Jew ever done to a Hungarian? Nothing... so why would they be denied the most meagre of mouthfuls of water, just a little to wet their lips.

Word passed from one mouth to the other, eyes opened up so they could all see the light at the end of the tunnel, where each would receive their dyer need, the substance that would drive their thirst from them.

Their throats burned and itched, and couldn't take any food in a lot of cases, unless it was in the form of soup, but no soup was to be had: so sore they were. But something had to be done in order to receive a little solace, even if for just a few hours where their throats would feel the benefit of their risk-taking.

The masses of Jews so desperate to wet their mouths congregated around several of the entrances to the huts and then rushed for the source of their desire, a water point not so very far away, a little clear ground around it but fairly close to several barracks where shelter could be sought if the guards were to come running with whips in hand and bayonets fixed. It was also true that there was safety in numbers and the likelihood of being targeted was less when there were more people around.

The rush of humanity came upon the ground, so sacred it was, for it held water, the clear essence of every man, woman and child, the liquid gold which couldn't be lived without, the daily requirement for which the body desired and screamed out for.

Guards then swamped the mass of humanity and commenced to hit them with the butts of their rifles, and others still got their sticks and whips and did what they could to cause more misery, but this was nothing to what the Hungarians in the towers around proceeded to do, and from out of one of the lookouts came several voices and these were followed by the cracking and thumping of ammunition being fired from rifles.

The Hungarians had begun shooting from high above, shooting at the unprotected and the weak, gazing through their sites in order to hone their shooting skills.

Two Hungarians laughed and shared a cigarette as they took turns in the killing, watching their victims fall without mercy, as the soldiers squeezed their triggers and inhaled another mouthful of smoke.

The SS below were a little shocked, too, for they were in the fray which was being caused and so the guards quickly adhered to the threats from above and pulled back, corralling the innocent in order for them to become easier targets for the Hungarians.

Medislaw and Vladislaw, two kapos with similar cast ideas of what it meant to be a man in power, were lined up with the SS guards and released their flurrying blows, bringing their whips down hard upon the head of those thirsty for water and too weak to fight back: but what did it mean to fight back, but bunker.

"Look at me, look at me now," said one guard to another as he drew his eye up against the iron sights of his rifle and with a smile upon his face he shot in the back a young girl who had joined her mother in an effort to get something to drink, to fill a small vase with water so that they could help with the ailing health of their sick grandmother who was too frail to walk or speak.

The victim fell dead, a grimace of horror painted upon her face, and as she fell the kapo Medislaw whipped her over the head for no good reason and she continued to the ground with blood trickling from her entry wound.

"Help me, Vladislaw," pleaded Medislaw, for there were too many to beat with a single whip. He continued whipping as fast as his hand could deliver the blows. "They like the beating so much; they keep coming for more," and he laughed, for he considered it much fun to bring such calamity to bear upon the shoulders of so many. The power he held in his hand was uplifting him, providing him with a false sense of pride.

Another victim fell dead in front of Vladislaw and he yelled back to his friend, "I'm sorry Medislaw," and another was shot before him, an elderly man falling dead. Vladislaw laughed, the smile so thickly set upon his face that he was overcome with frenzy, "but I am up to my armpits with filth."

Clara, the mother of the fallen daughter, turned to urge her child along, but on seeing the space where she was, now vacant, felt a terrible surge of fear penetrate her from head to foot. The startled and shocked look upon her face was not seen by those that whipped or those in the tower as they picked off their victims one by one. Suddenly she saw her daughter laying upon the ground, being trodden on by those in mass hysteria.

"Zelda! Zelda! Oh no... my God; what has happened?" and she fell beside her daughter, bringing her into her lap as a kneecap from someone close by kicked her in the side of the neck, but she was quick to sit back up and cradle her child in her arms. She looked into her face, her eyes closed, her breathing having ceased. The mother knew her daughter was no more and it took all of her energy just to hold her in the lap of love.

Another push and a kick came her way and then an inmate fell upon Clara, pushing her to the ground, face thirst in the mud.

Clara got up again upon her knees and once more the congestion of everyone around forced her back into the ground where a mouthful of mud was choked upon and then spat out. She's suddenly clubbed in the back of the head and the kapo searched for another victim. A woman fell beside Clara, having been shot in the head, her brains stuck to the side of her face, the eyes still open and staring right through Clara's soul.

Clara found it hard to then drag herself out of the fray, where whippings and shootings continued on and on. She clawed her way to the closest hut, crying as she moved, crawling through the mud and then over another body as one of the Hungarians in the tower smiled and slapped his friend on the back, pointing to the dead, boasting on how well he delivered the shot to the neck.

Clara pushed on, the pain of her loss, the pain of the misery, the pain of the exhaustion, hunger, and anger, almost too much to bear, but she continued until she fell safely into the dark shroud created by the open doorway and was delivered safely out of harm's way.

Clara rolled over and looked out upon the group, several hundred people clambering for water, for help, for solace; but none of it came. All that was delivered was more death and further whippings from the kapos that watched on as shots were fired into the corralled inmates.

By the time it was over there were over two-hundred dead littering the ground and over the next few days more were to join them, for the Hungarians were always on the lookout for an easy target.

Clara didn't know what to think or feel. The horrors of what had just happened were beyond all contemplation; it was sheer ludicrous and a mass murder of the likes she would never forget, not for so long as she lived, and she didn't know how long that would be. She considered her thoughts and realised without too much difficulty that her life, too, would be over sooner than she wished.

Clara waited until all was quiet and then she made her way back to her hut where her grandmother was waiting for water.

"Ah, Clara," said the grandmother of Zelda, Engelina. "Did you get some water?"

"No, mother; I'm sorry," answered Clara.

"Oh, dear; I don't think I can last much longer. I need something to drink, just a little," said Engelina. "Please, Clara; for your mother; just a mouthful."

"You'll have to wait for the soup," said Clara but she knew that there would be none. She would have to chance her luck and return to the water point if she was to get anything to drink, and then, of course, she ran the risk of bunker or death.

"Clara," said Engelina. "Where's Zelda?"

"She's gone to another hut, to help a friend. She'll be back in a few days; yes, she will," and Clara looked blankly at the wall, the dark interior, and contemplated death or possibly deliverance, deliverance from this hell hole called Bergen-Belsen. She craved for the day when the war would be over and all of those responsible for her daughter's death were brought to justice, and whether she lived to see that day or not, it mattered little, so long as justice was served.

CHAPTER 37

That night, in the silence that grew in the minds of all, the SS guards in a vast majority of cases were exchanged in place by Hungarian soldiers, continued on from the night before, the towers that sat so prominently around the camp being maintained throughout the night and not deserted for a second.

The shooting of the prisoners by an Hungarian the day before was nothing for a soldier of the SS. To him it was what must be endured, what was deserved, what was to be. In the eyes of German soldiers they were nothing more than stinking Jews, so why should they care that the Hungarians wished to practise their shooting skills. There was so little room in the camp already that the continuing slaughter was seen as a favour to those still alive.

One man had died during the night and he was seen as a pest. Someone had to now shove him outside, to be picked up by those who carted away the dead, but the reality was that there were so many dead that the collection of the bodies no longer continued. It was therefore up to the individuals to see to it that the dead were turned over to the mountain of flesh; but it was so far to walk.

A couple of men, thin and hungry, exhausted and slow, handled the body carelessly but managed to get it stowed beneath the floorboards, floorboards which had been loosened for the very need that engulfed the barracks. One of the two men considered leaving him where he lay until morning, to then shove him out into the cold morning air, but so be it to say that neither of them could give a damn anymore: wasn't it enough that they slaved to bury him beneath loose floorboards?

It took forever to haul the body into place and then drop it unceremoniously beneath the hut, to then cover it over so as to be unseen by the naked eye, and as the last of the floorboards was placed back into position there was a thunderous noise coming from somewhere outside. Somewhere in the camp was a commotion that couldn't be explained, and screams so terrifying that they could never be repeated did fill the night air, reverberating right throughout the area. It was so loud and heinous that it could be heard all the way down at the panzer school.

Blank faces looked from one to the other. What was it? What was happening? Was it the allies? Have they arrived at the camp?

A fellow inmate fell into the barrack and coughed loudly. He collapsed and tried to get his breath. He was unsettled but fell into the space made vacant by the old man that had just recently died, the bed space still available, for the two men on the same bunk didn't have the energy to roll over.

Jacob finally calmed himself and the coughing was abated, it was then that another from the opposite bunk opened his eyes from where he lay and asked the new-comer a question.

"What has happened?" asked Robert.

Jacob collected his thoughts and although he didn't feel like saying anything, commenced to tell his story, for he didn't want anyone else to fall victim to the malicious Hungarian soldiers who roosted upon the highpoints all around the camp.

"I have just witnessed something so terrible that it should not be spoken of," advised Jacob. "But I'll tell everyone here, whether they have the energy to listen to me or not, that the Hungarians are worse scum than the SS guards; far worse they are."

"Tell me," said Robert. "I'm listening."

"I don't know if I can. I might fall asleep as I tell you."

"It doesn't matter; I'll be asleep before you finish."

"Very well," said Jacob and he commenced with his story. "The Hungarian guards have dealt a vicious hand to hundreds of prisoners. They don't care whether they are old or young, woman or man; it matters not a shred to them," and he coughed some more before returning to the story. "The guards left the main gate open and organised for a kapo to lay a visit to several of the huts. The word was passed around that we were free, free to go about departing the camp. We were told that we were no longer prisoners and that the allies were so close that they were within walking distance. Many of us didn't believe them but others, those that had gone mad, listened and took heed."

"There are so many insane about," agreed Robert. "So many that they can't be counted."

"I can count them, count all of those in my hut that were mad with the desire to be free. More than 400 of them. They took the bait against better advice and strolled as best they could towards the open gate. It was then that a Hungarian officer took charge, and in complete ignorance to the Geneva Convention he ordered that the guards open fire with their machine guns. They are dead now, all of them. They were running in all directions, in the dark, the spotlights from the towers shining upon them and the machine-gunners kept on firing. There was some sniper fire too, men in the towers making the most of the opportunity they'd been given."

"They aren't men," said Robert.

"Yes, you are right. A man would not do what the Hungarians have done. The SS, yes, they would have done it."

"It was probably by order of the SS," said Robert.

"An order from Kramer himself," added Jacob. "I didn't know anyone that had fallen; not well in any case; just a few acquaintances, but the sheer slaughter of it all, it's too much to bear. I was lucky to get out the back of the hut for fear that they might come through and kill everyone."

"Why? Why did they do it?" asked Robert.

"It was a punishment for someone having stolen some bread."

"Who; who would steal from the Hungarians and be so stupid enough to be seen?"

Jacob was silent and the silence of the night told it all.

"So that is why you are here?"

"Don't turf me out," pleaded Jacob.

"I don't have the energy to," said Robert, "and besides, you cannot be blamed for being hungry; it isn't your fault; you're just stupid for being caught."

"Yes, you're right. Thank you," said Jacob. "Thank you for

listening. It means a lot to me."

"What will you do tomorrow?" asked Robert.

There was no answer.

"Are you asleep, Jacob?" asked Robert again of the new member of their hut.

The man beside Jacob answered for him. "No, Robert; he is dead; he's been shot. He has blood seeping from his back."

"I see it now," said Robert. "He was one of those who tried to make it out of the gate."

"Why would he be so stupid?"

"Because he is like most of us here; he is insane."

CHAPTER 38

On April 14th, the front lines of the advancing allies could be tasted, and the smell of liberation was in the air; everyone was hearing stories that the British would be upon them soon, and that a man dressed in British uniform had been seen just the day before, walking in the camp as though belonging to it. It would do well to be dressed in something warm and comfortable for when they arrived, for the journey back to one's own county would be a long and a hard one.

A man so close to death was walking beside the mass of bodies when he suddenly collapsed, falling upon the many that had fallen before him, in the heap of dead that skirted the fringe of the mountain. He was dead, life escaped, and there were a pair of eyes that saw him fall, but they were too slow in action for there was further movement. And then another old man came upon the scene, having not noticed the first fall the way he had, and neither did he know of the pair of eyes that were watching his every movement.

The old man was wandering about without concern or a cause and then with such great fortune fell upon the prize which was a gift from God himself. There before him was an overcoat upon a body, having gone seemingly unnoticed by the many. He, as quickly as he could, stripped the clothing from the body, the thick coat which was now his. He looked wearily around to ensure that no SS, Hungarian, or regular soldier, was watching his move. There was no hesitation in his action for he had no idea how long the war would go on for, or even that it would end, but he had to give it a fighting chance. Who was he to lay down his life willingly? Wasn't it God's will that each and every man should fight for his right to live? Wasn't it God who would simply take his life when He wanted it.

He wore the coat back to the hut and climbed upon his bunk before collapsing into a sleep from which he woke in the middle of the evening, for he had been followed by another that was witness to his good fortune and that person was now disturbing him. It was his nephew, a much younger man than himself.

The nephew liked the coat, liked what he saw, and understood that his uncle, the old man, would die before him. It was simple knowledge of the way things worked in Bergen-Belsen: the sick and the frail, in particular the old, mostly died first.

It was a sad case of affairs, but almost everyone was dressed in mere rags which rot on their bodies and were filled with lice. Men did all they could, in the end, to ensure their survival.

The nephew calmed the old man and pulled the coat from his shivering body, looking from left to right to ensure that no one saw him. He knew the British were coming and he needed something warm to wear in order to get away from the camp as quickly as possible, and the red spots on his arms were clear indication that he had typhus.

"Come, uncle," said the young man. "Give me the coat. I need it more than you. What are you going to do with it, ah?"

The old man couldn't fight, for he was too weak, but struggle a little he did, and during the course of being stolen from, said not a single word.

The nephew placed the coat on proudly as the uncle looked up from his spot upon the bunk. He was so very sad to see one of his own steal from him. The look in his face showed the true sadness of it all. He didn't cry, he didn't complain, but struggling a little was all he could do, but even then he had tired quickly and so the nephew took with relative ease, what wasn't his to take.

The nephew had stolen from the uncle and the uncle would now perish in the cold of the night, so close to liberation, but death was closer, and that night he died in the misery of the knowledge that his own family had denied him the right to live. The nephew felt no remorse at all; it was a matter of survival. It was a simple calculation: he had many years of life left to live, and the old man had but few.

This was the scenario seen over and over again, where behaviour was more in tune to that of wolves in the wild than human beings, but weren't human beings animals: and here before them all was the proof. The nephew would have to live with what he had had, would have to forgive himself for his transgressions upon his very own family later on in life. There was no justice in what he had done but in the nephew's eyes he was simply assuring that he survived, knowing that the old man, his uncle, would be dead soon enough, even if liberated he would soon be dead, for the old man's arms had more red spots than he.

The nephew snuck back to his bunk and put the coat on before clambering into his place beside two others. They were happy of his find, happy that he had a coat, for they too, could share in his good fortune by snuggling close to him, and if the nephew was to die then they would see to it that he was disrobed in an instant.

There didn't seem to be blatant murder between the inmates but their actions upon one another were causes that contributed to death all the same. The men and women of the camp weren't murderers, but many of them were guilty of manslaughter in some small way.

CHAPTER 39

On the night of April 14th, the SS guards congregated and discussed their situation.

The allies were coming and it wasn't going to be a friendly encounter. The SS guards would never allow themselves such an easy capture, in particular where there were so many living witnesses to the crimes they had committed over the past few years; even those SS that were relatively new to the camp had committed crimes against humanity, crimes which were against the Geneva Convention.

The guards had gathered together an assortment of clothing and soon found themselves drowned in friendly chatter and conversation as each and every one of them dressed themselves in civilian clothing.

They were talking, laughing, and sharing cigarettes.

Rucksacks were packed full of food, food meant for the prisoners of the camp. What did they care, they were to escape, never to be caught. So a few more Jews would die; it didn't matter to them, not in the least.

Each man helped himself to the platters of bread and cheese, provided for by Kramer himself, a little reward for the devotion that the SS guards had paid him and the camp's higher authority, which included Hitler himself, of course. There was even a framed photograph of Hitler to be seen hanging from the wall: all commandants with brown noses had a picture of Hitler on their wall.

Kramer, the cunning dog he was. The entire exercise of dwindling numbers of SS guards at post was one of his small ideas, an exercise to divert the attention away from the prying eyes of the camp that something was about to happen. It never occurred to him that the inmates of the camp were more concerned for their well-being and safe return home than the disappearance of the SS guards. Either way, be it in bulk or one at a time, the inmates of the camp were simply overjoyed to hear that the allies were on their way, but they kept the joy from being displayed in the open, hence they be shot, or given bunker and fed to the dogs.

The SS had stayed clear of the barracks and let no one see them when they attended the meeting with their commandant, and Kramer gave them all a hearty farewell speech which was applauded by the SS guards in unison; they were pleased to see that their efforts were appreciated.

Some of the prisoners were suspicious of the approaching liberation, which was spoken of but not guaranteed, and so few knew the truth that their word couldn't be counted upon as being true, but because some of the SS had been seen and overhead to be talking amongst themselves several of the inmates drew up plans for their departure and the arrival of the British.

Some of the inmates knew something was up, felt it in their bones, and small groups of them got together to talk on what measures they should take in regards to the running of the camp once the allies arrived. Bergen-Belsen should be run by them, the slaves of the Third Reich. This camp had been their torturous home and the time would come soon enough when they would have to deal with an uncertain future and see to it that their people were cared for. What better way to do this than run the administration of the camp for themselves.

The allies would have done their duty by liberating the camp and the inmates would be truly grateful for that, and each of the elders within the camp knew that the more help that they could provide to the allies in regards to the administration of the camp, a camp they knew inside out, the more it would free the liberators of the most meaningless tasks. It was crucial to all those in Bergen-Belsen that over the days after the British entered their domain that they would be able to get on with their duty and hunt down those murderous antagonist bastards known as the SS.

The SS guards, on the other hand, knew a little about tactics, knew that they were relatively a small group and could be easily found in the few days after the arrival of the British, and with this knowledge they devised a plan. In order to hide their tracks they would endeavour to employ the assistance of others and so the call went out to all of those that had helped with the running of the camp, for the more there were to hunt down, the better their chances of escape. Many kapos rallied to the call and prepared to make good their escape with the SS, alongside their compatriots, seeing this as their last opportunity to escape from the crimes they'd committed against humanity. It was an escape from their convictions of death.

The kapos were too dim-witted to know what was going on in the mind of Kramer and his SS guards, but they could taste the freedom which they also desired; they were happy to give up their daily whipping of the prisoners for this humble opportunity to escape with the SS guards, regardless of their previous torments.

And so, as the darkness of night continued, broken only by sirens of the night and the searchlights of war, the men who thrived on hatred, crawled off like dogs into the country, to try and evade their persecutions.

CHAPTER 40

On the Sunday afternoon of April 15th, 1945, the allies took control of the German Army Training Garrison – the Panzer Training School and barracks – which was situated one and a half kilometres down the road from Bergen-Belsen. A General headquarters was set up in this barracks with its lush surroundings appealing to the high-ranking officers who had not yet witnessed first-hand the squalor which was about to confront them, and chief members of staff met here to commence with organising the relief operation. The prisoners were now to also be referred to as internees; no longer prisoners of the Third Reich.

The Allied 21st Army Group was sufficiently pleased with the cooperation of the Germans thus far and the sight of the 15,000 internees maintained near the garrison, although an unpleasant scene that disgusted the British and Canadian soldiers, was nothing to what was about to be witnessed once the gates of Bergen-Belsen were entered.

The limits of the neutral territory were finalised and so were the basic ground rules for the treatment of the SS and regular soldiers currently guarding the concentration camp, ground rules which were to be awkwardly accepted in the face of what was about to come of age and history.

The 11th Armoured continued on their way and stopped momentarily on reaching the main gate of the camp, Bergen-Belsen, seeing several German officers awaiting the arrival of the British, before they continued on in their tanks, several remaining behind.

Several soldiers stepped from their vehicles and approached the fence, throwing up the contents of their stomachs on seeing what lay before them. They quickly returned to their vehicles and continued on their way, shaking from the horrible scene that had hit them like a mallet.

With their vehicle escort gone the British officers approached the main gate sided by an entourage of British soldiers, 240 in total, who were mostly apprehensive in regards to what they might find, for the state of the camp was deplorable from where they stood and beyond any reasonable explanation.

Josef Kramer smiled as he met Lieutenant Derrick Sington. Kramer was standing there in a fresh uniform at the entrance to the camp, the thoughts of the state of the camp going through his mind as he hoped, beyond all reasonable hope, that he'd be seen as a German who'd tried his utmost to save as many dying people as could be saved.

"I can only hope for an orderly transition," said Kramer as he stood there with 30 armed SS, some of which were female; miserable dogs not worth a penny. "I think what we need is cooperation between us. There is so much I can do to help you, in particular considering how well I know the camp and the prisoners. It is an unpleasant situation that we have here but I'm sure that the advice I have will do us well to overcome all that we are faced with, and I must warn you, that this camp contains professional criminals, political prisoners, and homosexuals."

From within the camp several shots were heard and Kramer was quick to provide further orientation by saying: "The prisoners are rioting and trying to force their way into the food storage facility. We have to open fire, sometimes; they leave us no choice."

The heat under the collar of one of the officers nearby was simply too much and he leant forward and in a vicious manner gave the commandant a warning. "We will shoot one SS man for every damn internee killed," and the look on Kramer's face did not change, and nor did the attempts on the part of the Germans to give aid to the former prisoners. Not a single German did anything more than was forced upon him when it came to helping the sick and wounded. There was no good cause for all of the starvation; the Germans were surrounded by farms of cattle, hens, geese, ducks and crops. There wasn't a German to be seen, for miles around, that went without a single meal.

Lieutenant-Colonel Taylor of the British Army then arrived, and having heard the shooting in the distance gave the order for those before him to be immediately disarmed, which the soldiers about him saw to immediately; at least some of the killing would stop, he thought, but for the time being the guards at their posts would remain armed and able to carry out their duties, but under a heavy, watchful eye.

Shortly after having met Josef Kramer and others at the camp entrance, the camp was entered by a group of officers, including Brigadier Llewelyn Glyn-Hughes, the medical officer in command of the relief operation.

Kramer was surrounded by MPs, showing the allies into the camp, taking his time to enable the destruction of the camp records within the reception area and other offices to continue, so they could be eradicated from existence, forever lost.

Some internees of exception, kept in isolation for so long, were also killed where they lay or dragged outside before the British even entered the camp, to be killed and thrown upon the pile of corpses which was five deep in most cases, if not more. The British, however, saw the plot in Kramer's actions and pressed on with the move of men to key points within the camp, to do what they could to prevent the destruction of documentation and personnel, each appointed man so tasked followed by their entourage of troops, and where applicable, several tanks.

The sights before them indicated the type of man that Kramer was and the scene painted the picture for what evidence was to be found, and if these criminals of war were ever to be brought to justice then the MPs and the others of the units currently present needed to move as quickly as possible.

There wasn't just the evidence, for that was superficial, but the men, women, and children needed to be saved. They were the witnesses and could give real evidence to what had happened within the camp. But death wasn't to be averted simply because of the inconvenience it would cause, of course not. These people deserved life, deserved better than to be treated in this poor fashion, and such a poor state they were all in that words could not convey the horrors of the camp to the fullest.

Nigel B.J. Clayton

Alongside Sington, of the 14th Amplifier Unit, came officers of Intelligence Corps and the 63rd Anti-Tank Regiment, Royal Artillery. A van with a loudspeaker and its crew, three of whom were Jewish, commenced immediately to convey their message of liberation, and despite the tears that welled in their eyes they continued to pass on the news that they, the internees, were now saved.

"You are free... you are free," came the voices of the liberators as they cast their message far and wide and in several different languages. The camp was known to comprise of Romanian, Polish, Yugoslav, French, Belgian, Russian, Czech, Greek, Hungarian and German people; Jews, Prisoners of War and criminals; just to name a few. They were from right across the face of Europe. "Food and medical aid will come; be calm."

The commander of the Anti-Tank Regiment, Lieutenant-Colonel Taylor, was flabbergasted as were all else that day, but he continued with the task of touring the camp as Derrick Sington continued reciting in German that the camp had been liberated and that the internees should, for the time being, remain where they were.

The sights and smells were literally too much to bear. The German estimates of sick could only be an outrageous underestimate. There were piles of dead; thousands of them; too many to be counted and each at a different degree of decomposition. Men and women staggered around the compound, some cheered, others collapsed. Some of the internees came wandering up the allies, their liberators, with smiles upon their pathetically thin faces, their outstretched arms nothing more than bone covered with skin of red sores and spots. Lice could be seen upon the heads of some, miniscule pests crawling in their thousands over their victims in great masses, so thick that it was impossible to believe. The further they entered the camp and the more the internees became aware, and a suffocation of humanity crowded in upon the British soldiers, trying in all their might to hiss and hug them.

Men and women pulled young sprigs from the birch trees that

140

grew alongside the road which divided the camp and flung them graciously upon the allies. One sprig fell upon Kramer's shoulder and he flicked it away in disgust.

A German soldier then fired several shots into the air, to give warning to those that clambered around, for the Jews to get out of the way and to restore order. Sington withdrew his pistol and on giving a warning for the soldier to cease his action the kapos that remained behind leapt to action and started beating the internees. It was a frightful sight that sickened every British soldier there, but nothing could be done at the present for the crowd was too thick and large.

But there was a job to be done and the reality of the camp must be pushed aside, and Llewellyn commenced to carry out his bidding.

The bodies were piled everywhere, and in some places it was hard to tell which were dead and which of those might still be alive, and harder still to tell the difference between a man and a woman, and movement could be seen amongst the piles of dead as though being 'nearly dead' was the same as 'being dead' and hence they were treated in the same way by those that were maintained in the camp.

Llewellyn moved closer for more clarity, to see for himself what manner of diseases might be prevalent in the camp, by looking over the dead, and he could clearly see, on closer inspection, that there was mass evidence of cannibalism in the camp. There were literally hundreds of bodies amongst the mountains of dead that had had their liver, kidneys and heart removed. It was such a sickening thought but as he looked around he thought, just for a fleeting moment, how it could be possible. People did all manner of strange things in order to stay alive.

Several of the wondering sick, skeletons of skin on bone, tripped over themselves and lay there upon the ground, unable to get up, and others who were more able, approached the liberators with arms outstretched, to hug the dear men that had come to save them from the Nazi Regime and the cold-blooded

Nigel B.J. Clayton

manner in which it viewed the rights of others to live freely.

As news spread of the liberation the soldiers became swamped by internees that resembled stick figures, everyone wishing to give thanks to the soldiers that had come to set them free.

CHAPTER 41

Overcrowding within Bergen-Belsen was taking its toll upon those imprisoned there, and the sheer lack of running water, food and medicine, simply added to the uncontrollable outbreak of typhus which had to date been blamed directly for the death of some 37,000 internees. Only now, with the liberators on the porch, was some reprieve to be received from the disease.

One such diseased person now approached a soldier of the British army, staggering with great difficulty towards the soldier who was horror struck by what he saw. It was Franzi, she came to tell the man about the dead marine, how the soldier of the British army had been ordered shot by Kramer himself. The soldier took the news directly to his commander and Franzi was given some special care, an apple to eat and some water. And as Franzi was being taken care of there was further movement in the camp. From elsewhere within, far from the main gate, something was stirring.

Groups of British soldiers were moving around and could just make out the scene quite some distance away as some internees had come together, moving out from their huts. Some of the internees were lining up as best as possible, many dead and dying still occupying the bunks of buildings or upon floors where bunks simply did not exist; but it was more than clear: the internees were dragging themselves from their huts by the thousands. It was the normal procedure for a roll call but so few parades had been held over the past few days; but it was simply instinct that they should line up to be counted?

Throughout the camp so large there was much evidence to show that the internees didn't know they had been liberated. Some were too weak, some were insane, and others refused to believe that they had been saved and felt deep down that it was all another ploy of the SS to have them killed for trying to escape.

But the internees could hear the noise growing around them. There was noise developing from outside the camp, not too far away. A few rifle shots could be heard and vehicles in the distance, tanks and armoured cars approaching from afar. The changing of gears could also be heard so it was evident that there was a truck nearby. Were they being moved to another camp? There were no SS guards to be seen, no one to do the count. And then some SS came to view, staff members, not guards – or so they say – but technicians and clerks, but in the eyes of the former prisoners these scum were as bad as one another; they were all guards, all guilty of punishing them when punishment was not just. Here they were, walking around the camp wearing white armbands as a sign of surrender to British and suddenly, there it was, a military vehicle that was not German, and so it had to have been British or American, possibly Russian even.

Most of the internees were far too weak to give celebration to the sight of the gates being opened and the entrance of the British as they came upon the unforgettable sight before them. These liberators were sickened to the core by what they saw and smelt. These men so hardened by battle were shaken to the bone.

Many battles had been fought, many dead contended with, but nothing like this Hell Camp had ever been encountered before. And as a few cheers went up and smiles appeared on faces for the first time in many years, so too did the feelings of degradation, for some of the soldiers that had come to give aid were bent over near the fence and throwing up whatever food was within them. Both sides of the fence were sickened, in different ways, but at least the internees were free.

Laughter commenced to grow, as too did the weeping, so many different emotions being felt all at the same time. The internees were simply... listless and lost. The sheer joy that was felt within these skeletons of human life was simply... so joyous. But even now as the British entered the camp, the SS that remained, along with the Hungarian guards, were shooting internees in the distance, for whatever reason they could find. Out of sight, out of harm's way, no witnesses to point a bony finger in their direction.

CHAPTER 42

British soldiers couldn't believe their eyes, the piles of dead that were decaying before them. The children's compound next to this main stretch weren't even spared the insanity of it all, where the naked bodies of men and women simply lay there rotting away, the stench filling the air for miles around.

The children had grown accustomed to the sight as had many of the adults, but for the children there was the added anxiety of not knowing if that figure upon the ground was their mother or aunt, and that man with the mark upon his face... was that father?

And the piles of dead were so steep in places that they involuntarily collapsed into the gutter alongside the street of the camp, disease to be carried away with rain when it came. There were even bodies hanging from the electric fences where people had thrown themselves quite deliberately to their death in order to be rid of the suffering which they had to endure. No matter where you looked, death was there and not a single soul, whether capable or not, attempted to remove a dead body in the middle of the road or a corpse that hung from a fence.

And then a man could be seen dragging himself upon the pile of corpses, dragging himself into position, to lay himself to rest. He felt dead already but had just enough energy to displace himself upon those that had passed this world for another filled with merit and salvation. He finally collapsed upon a comrade and the last of his breath escaped him as he died in front of the liberators, as they entered the camp to give relief to the multitudes.

It was indescribable, not in a thousand years could one give a precise description on what was discovered within the wire fences of Bergen-Belsen; not even a photograph could express the sheer horrors that were encountered. The gutters were full of corpses; the huts, too, were littered with dead, some of which were still lying next to the dying and sick. The British could see, quite easily, where the freshly filled mass-graves existed, one of which was still in the process of being filled. In huts where there were no bunks the bodies of men and women were curled up in balls for there was no room to lay out straight, no room to stretch, no space in which to roll over. How was it possible to fit one thousand people into a barracks or other building that was suited for no more than one hundred, and how many huts were there? There were more than a hundred huts altogether.

The world would be shocked to hear of Bergen-Belsen, and as the liberators went about their duties the world around continued as it did. The birds were flying in the sky as normal, here as in any other place upon the face of the earth, and Germans living down the road denied knowing anything of the horror camp, saying that they didn't know anything about it, that they couldn't smell the death of the camp. How was it that thousands upon thousands of German citizens didn't know what was going on near their own town; it was absurd?

CHAPTER 43

Lieutenant-Colonel Taylor returned to the front gate and ordered that all the SS be arrested and placed under guard in their barracks; the killing had to be stopped and someone needed to be answerable for the condition of the camp.

The Military Police had wasted no time at all in positioning themselves at what was unanimously considered as the entrance to the camp, monitoring all those that entered and exit with good cause, although the last thing that the military wished for was for typhus to be spread by those wandering the neutral zone and further afield, and so, although liberated, a vast majority of the internees weren't so confident as to think of themselves as free.

The internees were wondering around, dazed and confused, for no good reason, as though their minds were empty of any sane thought, walking blindly here and there, some becoming startled on hearing the banging of pots, and so came the order from the MPs at the gate that adhesive tape should be placed over vehicle horns, to prevent anyone from pressing them, for some internees were so fragile that the blast from a horn could surely kill them as easily as could the malnutrition and disease.

A few more officers, very late in arrival, then approached the main gate to the horror camp.

As they approached the entrance to Bergen-Belsen they could smell the rotting flesh, even though it was just momentarily experienced, for the wind had died down to but a whisper of its former April zest.

"I heard that a little blame came our way in regards to the lack of medical supplies and food," said one officer, "our aircraft doing a marvellous job at spoiling the supply lines."

"Yes; I heard similar."

"But did you hear of the latest report?"

"No. What is that?"

"The Germans cut the supply of water themselves, and even sabotaged the electricity to the camp."

"Those bastards will have to answer for that."

CHAPTER 44

An officer in SS uniform could be clearly seen quite some distance off, standing over an internee who had sunk to their knees, seemingly pleading for clemency, asking for a slice of bread and forgiveness in the wake of their graduation from prisoner to internee. The SS officer lifted his arm and within the clenched fist of his hand could be seen a whip, its lashings flying through the air, knots evident along its strips of leather in order for it to cause much pain and misery as it was cast down upon a Jew.

A British soldier sprang to action and ran across the ground littered with bodies of the dead and the walking insane; of those sane enough to search for clothing, food and water, and those simply staggering around looking for relatives or a helping hand.

A few startled stares were cast his way, looking upon him in wonder, unsure of what he was about, and a few internees felt somewhat afraid that they had done something wrong and that the liberator was out to do them harm. But the soldier forged ahead, forgetting his place, forgetting absolutely that the last thing needed was for those of the camp to be startled in any way.

Damned if you did, and damned if you didn't; but from deep within the British soldier escaped a simple command: "Stop acting like a savage."

The soldier with white arm band, a signature that he'd surrendered to the allies, thrust down upon the innocent Jew several more times before looking up at the armed liberator as he closed the gap.

The SS officer had no weapons other than the whip he'd just taken was a shelf within an office and a sidearm which he was permitted to carry. Others, in particular the Hungarians upon the towers surrounding the camp, carried rifles and were well equipped to inflict great damage where needed, and several of these men watched from above as the scene unfolded before them.

The British soldier was taking a chance with destiny and luck but those upon the towers around the camp didn't dare to think twice of bringing fire to bear upon him. Killing a Jew was one thing for the Hungarians to do, but to shoot dead a British soldier when white bands were worn by them all was not worth thinking about. So the prying eyes of the Hungarians in view of the commotion simply turned a blind eye and they continued smoking their cigarettes.

The Geneva Convention was represented in all quarters, treaties and protocols that protected all people from atrocity, but the concentration camps seemed to be free of this encumbrance, but the SS officer in particular should have known better. There could be no denying the facts. This inhuman behaviour was nothing compared to the truth of the years of abuse but was enough for the British soldier to forget himself that minute as he arrived upon the scene and lashed out with a fist upon the face of the officer.

The SS officer fell upon the ground, shocked slightly by what had just occurred, but not because of what the liberator had done to him, but because he realised, just then, that he was powerless to do anything about it.

The internee could not believe what had just happened. One moment he was being whipped by an officer of the SS and the next the officer was drawing his hand from his face, seeing if blood had been spilt. The internee could not believe that the might of the SS had been subdued by the free hand of a British soldier so easily.

And from near the entrance of the gate the commotion that had drawn quite a lot of attention was immediately conveyed from man to man and the situation in regards to the guards in the towers being permitted to bear arms was taken into consideration. The British simply could not take the risk of the Hungarians opening fire upon them, for the internees were telling stories that chilled British blood.

Another British soldier then looked up towards one of the gates to the camp and saw several of the internees staggering out

149

of the campgrounds, in obvious search for food. They might be carrying typhus and here they were, walking freely from the camp. The Hungarian soldiers cared little, smoking their cigarettes and not even attempting to look up or stop the two from walking past them and into freedom.

The disease had to be contained, and so the soldier did all he could and reported to his officer in command.

The soldier and an officer with translator beside them then approached the offending Hungarian at the gate, quick action being called for, and as they approached they saw an old woman wrapped in a blanket. She stood talking with the Hungarian guard but all he did was shrug his shoulders and she kept on walking.

The officer and translator spoke with the guard as the soldier retrieved the old woman. The Hungarian told the translator that the old woman was going home to Poland and he started to laugh before being ordered to put out his cigarette, which he did on realising that he was outnumbered and in the wrong.

CHAPTER 45

That late afternoon, Commandant Josef Kramer was taken by the British Military Police, under arrest and removed, and as he was being escorted out of his office he could see that much fury was being unleashed as British troops took vengeance upon several Germans, who were fallen upon with rifle butts and stabs with bayonets.

The power had clearly shifted from the axis to the allies and there was nothing that he could do to slow it. It was turning into a forceful handover, no nicety about it. A swift hand was better than a swift word and the British would not take lightly to any incursion or mistreatment against a helpless internee. Enough was enough and further atrocity was to be curbed immediately.

The commandant was completely unashamed of what surrounded him, didn't care at all about what he had created, and it seemed that he had no idea of what he had caused. The camp was rife with typhus, but typhus had caused far fewer deaths than starvation. How on earth could the staff of the camp be so fat if there was no food to be had? Kramer was taken straight to the Panzer barracks and locked away, to be interrogated over the coming days; the answers to be extracted from him one way or another.

And so the orders were drawn rather quickly after the British entered the camp, seeing for themselves the state of affairs they had voluntarily accepted, and knowing that Kramer was safely locked away it was now time for action, action, action. There was to be no sitting around and doing nothing. Every man available, regardless of rank, was to be kept busy with his duty. There wasn't a moment to lose.

It was a matter for survival that a massive rescue plan be put into action, the heights of which had never been seen before, to the memory and knowledge of all, and should be carried out immediately and without a second being wasted.

The German barracks down the road at the training facility, where 15,000 internees were currently being cared for and released of their shackles, would be employed well as they were modern buildings of brick and well equipped. Not only could they provide shelter to the internees suffering so badly, but they were clean and free of faeces and lice. Such a commodity as this barracks would be put to great use, more so than could possibly be imagined; no longer a haven for which to store men of war but now a secure location for which to help cure the sick.

As the liberation came into full swing it became all the more clearer to the prisoners that they had been liberated, were now known as internees, and that each and every one of them wished to seek food or contend themselves with having it delivered to them. There were currently no obvious rules in place for the delivery of food or water and so the internees seemed to feel as though they had been left to fend for themselves.

Several British troops were hence faced with a dilemma, and that was that the human wave before them wished to ransack the kitchens for every single ounce of food the internees could get their hands upon. But in order for the entire camp to be fed there was to be an orderly manner about them. The British troops, therefore, had little option but to hold back the mass of people by firing warning shots over their heads in the hope that some form of control could be maintained.

Some of the internees, even before that action to call them to order was carried out by the British, felt as though they were still prisoners, still held against their will. To them the British were just another problem to contend with. Again they were being dealt a vicious hand, shots being fired to see them submit to orders: from one state of depressing affairs to another... it seemed the way of all things.

The British didn't wish to waste any time at all in their efforts to provide everyone with proof of freedom, to show that they were there to help; to feed the internees, water them, provide medical assistance and the means for each and every one of them to get back home, to begin again their lives with any loved ones that had managed to survive this great ordeal... this pestilence of man.

Here in this camp, the shock of its very existence, rocked every man and far excelled all of the experienced horrors combined, from all of the battles over the past 12 months and more, from all the way from Normandy to Bergen-Belsen. This was a place like no other, a camp of appalling squalor where disease was rampant, nothing more than the true symbol of Nazi hatred and the barbarity which simply couldn't be fathomed. sixty-thousand internees, dead or alive; they were still human beings.

CHAPTER 46

Needless to say the liberators needed somewhere to house the men that were to carry out their mission in saving the poor souls of Bergen-Belsen, and so the lengthy execution of their right to expel residents from the nearby towns was enacted.

The internees in particular would be invited later to come and go as they pleased from the confiscated houses that the liberators took from the Germans, if they were free of disease, to take what they wanted from the German civilians, to take from those fighting against the allies; and some of the town was set on fire, to be watched as the houses crumbled and burnt to the ground.

Another soldier came up to relieve one of the officers on duty and indicated that the officer was to report immediately to the next highest in rank. He reports and hears that several houses along the street nearest the camp entrance have been taken from the owners, the owners dispatched with an almighty shove. This was to be his place of residence until such a time that the officer was advised that it was time to move on.

Tables and chairs within this house were beautiful and there was a basket of fruit placed in the centre of a dresser. It is hard to understand how such beauty could be in existence, where fresh fruit was available at arm's length, all in such close proximity to a camp filled with rampant disease and squalor of the likes never seen before in the history of man. How was it possible that German citizens could sit back in leisure, their faces full of food, when such degradation existed not so far away? There was no good reason or excuse. The civilian population were as much to blame for the conditions of Bergen-Belsen as the SS guards themselves.

Whilst the German citizens passed their days in good health, the Jews of Bergen-Belsen were living in hell. As the civilians grew stronger the Jews grew sicker, weaker, thinner. Some of the internees were so deteriorated on the day of liberation that nothing more could be done for them and so they would be overlooked for treatment. Doctors would mark a red cross on the foreheads of those whom they thought had any possibility of surviving, for there was no time to waste on those closest to death when others could be saved.

Repatriation was sought by two, for Holland. The young woman who went by the name of Eta accepted her card on giving her details, and as her elderly father then gave his to the British officer at his post.

Eta tried holding onto the old man for fear he might fall, but as he handed his card over to the British officer, he collapsed without warning.

"No! Father," cried Eta as she fell beside him, holding his head from the ground, where it was foul and stinking. "Don't die, not now. We are saved."

The British officer felt the weight of the pain but there was nothing he could do; there was far too much work to be done and so he ordered a private to move in and help Eta out of the way, so that others could log their details and commence with their repatriation.

The private picked the father up with Eta still clinging to him and the body was carried to the side of the tent where the weeping continued. The old man was easy to lift, didn't weigh much at all, and the private could feel the old man's bones – they were like sticks of wood, branches to be thrown upon a fire; kindling perhaps. He was so thin. The private then thought of himself and wondered whether or not he'd catch some sort of disease; possibly typhus, but he only needed to look around him before he realised that there is more at stake than his health, and besides, there were doctors and nurses to treat him if he required it. There was an entire civilization here that needed help, an entire city at his fingertips that was dying before him. There are so many in need that he didn't care about the few lice that fell upon his sleeve.

And so the father died, then and there, having fallen to the ground, dead.

Eta broke down and cried some more for her father but all the tears in the world would not bring him back. So close to real freedom and his life was stolen from him. But it was his willingness to see freedom and liberation that kept him going in the first place. He saw his daughter receive freedom, witnessed her being saved, and that's all he ever wanted. What more could a parent ask for their child?

A priest from Canada passed by Eta and on seeing her being cared for by a soldier he continued on and went amongst the masses, to help where he could; he was Reverence Ted Aplin.

A soldier with a beret also saw the grief stricken girl, a soldier of the 63rd Anti-Tank regiment. He has come in to seek family, he was a relative of one of the internees, and on seeing the deplorable state of affairs began to help where he could, his relatives forgotten as he continued to give aid to those in need.

Twenty-seven water carts then arrived at the camp and a small portion of those having not seen fresh water for so long got to have a drink; like thirsty cattle they were drawn to the containers of water as though able to smell it. Word travelled fast amongst them and soon the entire area was swarming with people wanting to quench their thirst and to take back what they could for those unable to move from their bunks.

Soldiers were billeted outside the camp so that they were close enough to enter camp each day, close enough to serve, as best they could, those that should be served, for not all soldiers were given quarters to live in: not all soldiers had sufficient rank, and so it was for them that they experience the most of the misery within the fenced off areas of Bergen-Belsen.

That first night was one of tension. It was feared that the internees would try to kill every SS soldier in the camp as well as raid the stores for food, and the fears were well considered. Sherman tanks were brought in to give clear warning to those in the camp, and a cordon was placed around the buildings of concern. Nevertheless, by morning all food stores were gone, the SS stores facility had been ransacked, every single turnip in the camp had vanished, and Kramer's personal pen of 25 pigs had disappeared without a trace, not a single sow's ear to be seen.

CHAPTER 47

How was it that the lost dignity of so many years could be restored? It needed to be built, one brick at a time, but done in such quick fashion that not another person would die after this day, but such a vision was too far from the reality of the situation, and all that could be done, was being done.

This was April 16th, and there was much work to be continued and arranged.

The water supply was turned back on and many of those capable now washed themselves unashamedly as best they could, naked and in full view of other internees and soldiers alike, washing themselves clean for the first time in as long as most could remember. And where did the energy come from to carry out such a task, but from the very dignity that they had already been provided, even if it meant washing butt naked in front of so many strange men of the British army?

A DDT truck entered the compound and via the Amplifier Unit instructions were passed around for those available to gather around. It was time to take care, once and for all, the horror of the dreaded lice infestations which had bred itself out of control. Every single person was covered in sores and itches, lice prevalent no matter where one chose to look.

The delousing program commenced immediately and like snow from heaven the white dust settled upon the bodies of those that had managed to get themselves out of doors and into the breeze of the cold afternoon, those that were not desperately sick. Soon they were all covered in white but the remarkable effect of the cure had its way with all, for the lice dropped like the bodies of men, falling from the heads and armpits of those that carried them. It was a true godsend that, at least, some of the torment of their existence had now been eradicated from their lives; if only the SS could so easily be eradicated.

The British were working as hard and as fast as they possibly could, but even at the rate in which they worked it took two weeks before the entire camp was deloused sufficiently. Fresh clothing, confiscated from nearby German homes, sometimes at gunpoint, was provided to those of the camp and they started to feel as though this really was the end of their misery. Gone were the rags and prisoner uniforms, the striped flannel garments and pyjamas, but again, the transition from one to the other took much time and patience.

CHAPTER 48

The women guards were taken to work, to help bury the dead and the decaying, paraded by the British as they were marched to work past the survivors of the camp, those Jews lucky enough to see liberation being delivered.

Needless to say the cowardly lot protested in the way that they were treated, to be escorted in front of the Jews and made to work by burying the dead. A British sergeant then screamed out to them, in
good German, that they had created the mess before them and so they should clean it up.

But it wasn't just the women that saw swift justice fall upon them. The Hungarian guards, too, felt the brunt of hatred being dealt to them from the British liberators. It was the sheer shock and disbelief that confronted the allies that turned them into issuing their own punishments and in some cases this was metered out in large quantities, being as severe as it was deserved.

There was refusal on the part of a Hungarian officer to allow himself or his four men to handle the dead as it was against the Geneva Convention to be forced into such labour, and he seemed to have forgotten the four hundred that he had ordered be shot just several nights before.

The British captain in charge then advised the Hungarian, in short, that he was under martial law and could be charged with mutiny, or dealt swift punishment before it being heard by a court. The officer again refused to do as he was ordered.

The captain, having heard enough, the smell of the dead pressing upon him, the sights and sounds closing in upon him, then drew out his revolver and on cocking it did hold the weapon at the Hungarian officer's head and repeated one last time that he should order his men to work and get busy with helping them bury the dead.

The Hungarian again refused to accept the terms of the order and was summarily shot in the head without a further word being spoken. The other four Hungarian soldiers then rushed the captain who stood his ground and watched as eight British soldiers, four either side, opened fire with their sten guns, killing the former guard's dead.

The captain then ordered the soldiers to throw the bodies in the mass grave, along with the Jews, and reported to his superior what he had done. The colonel then replied to the captain's admittance that he had done the internees a service and saved the hangman the dirty task of taking their lives.

Eta was looking for her father but his body couldn't be found; she'd lost him after collapsing the day before, the emotions of the loss forced upon her being too much. His body was amongst the other dead and she searched continuously, but it was useless. The sadness of the situation was unbearable, unthinkable and unacceptable. It was now that she blamed the liberators for gross incompetence before again breaking down and crying. She wept for so long that she fell asleep amongst the dead.

A Hungarian soldier then came up and started to pull on her leg, to drag her to the mass grave that awaited her body. She opened her eyes and stared up at the soldier who was being watched by a man in British uniform.

"I'm not dead yet," said Eta. "Please, have patience."

CHAPTER 49

Two officers were walking, mid-afternoon, from the Panzer barracks towards the camp, a walk of just over a kilometre in distance, and where the wind came from a direction other than from the camp, it was quite wonderful. There were trees all over and there were also patches of ground where the trees had been taken for use in the kitchens, even the roots having been dug from out of the ground.

As the officers walked along the road and into the camp, having passed many others in pursuit of their work and errands, a priest came to view, who had perched himself upon an altar which had been made from several boxes and a red curtain whose demeanour had seen better days when hung up in the halls of the luxury barracks some distance behind the officers.

The priest was giving a sermon to several members of the internees whose state was so poor that it appeared that many of them were accepting this mass as their last: their last rights.

And as the priest continued with what he knew best the unfortunate pressed ever towards him, hunched forward or on their hands and knees, to take into their mouths the blessing being provided. For some this would be the last day on earth and by sunrise they would be dead.

It was a wonder in itself that these people, regardless of religion, had sought to praise God in all his glory, even as death pressed against them. What did these people owe God for their mistreatment? Where was God when they needed him most? But for the strong the answers were obvious, for the Third Reich was being stripped of its glory and embellishments, and was crumbling to its foundation.

It was true; the good would always prosper over evil, no matter how long it took. It was obvious in all this war upon war, this killing upon killing, that God was indeed their saviour. Good had won over evil in the past and would do so again in the future; the good would always prosper, in the end, over the insanity of the fanatic. Evil should never again be given the opportunity to deliver such heinous punishment against the innocent; and one of the two officers looked at the other as the priest continued his sermon, even in the face of the fact that another priest from within the camp itself lay dead upon the ground before him, having done his best in providing healing to those in need; and the officer said to his comrade, "They crawl from so far. They should be preserving their energy. The sermons should be taken to the sick, not the sick coming to the sermon."

And even as they spoke the victims of Hitler's cruelty could be seen dragging themselves towards the makeshift altar.

"Yes, indeed," said the second. "I would never have believed that one human being could cause such depravity to fall upon another. This atrocity had to be shouted to the world, for all to hear; it simply shouldn't be allowed to happen again. Perhaps our efforts here will be the preventative measure needed to safeguard the innocent of the future."

The first officer locked eyes with his companion and said, "Yes, wouldn't it be grand; but I fear you are mistaken."

CHAPTER 50

Water tankers and three-tonne trucks with cooking equipment arrived late in the afternoon, food and more water too, and it was then that the internees were ordered back to their barracks so that the distribution of food could be conducted. Aid was sought from those internees that were able to move around and so commenced the feeding of the camp.

Yet the vast majority of the people en mass was still so weak that they did little to help themselves, and soldiers unaware of the true epidemic in terms of people's abilities left food for those within the huts on doorsteps and entrances. But the food wasn't touched and those inside continued to die as they'd died the day before and the week before that.

The food consisted of such nourishment, and the internees had not seen food or eaten for so long, that the very goodness of it all made them feel sick and was the direct cause why so many fell dead shortly after liberation, to no fault of the liberators themselves.

Army rations were the main source of their initial diet for there simply wasn't anything else immediately available; it was simply too rich for their digestive systems to handle and much diarrhoea was again suffered by almost everyone within the camp, and where diarrhoea was alleviated, vomiting usually took its place. No matter what, the food that went in was coming back out, be it via the front entrance or the rear.

Men and women alike, although the children of the adjoining compound were far better off, simply scooped up what food they could, taking it into their mouths and then finding that it was almost impossible to swallow. The ulcers within their mouths were such a great hindrance that convulsions accompanied the swallowing of food; it simply could not be avoided.

Two thousand perished over the next few days due to being fed the incorrect food. The internees were at different levels of malnutrition; some could stomach food and others could not. You're damned if you ate and damned if you didn't. Much more work was needed in considering the diets of those most in need, but time was not on the allies' side.

And how did the liberators feel, providing good food to the internees to then see them curl up and die in pain over the next few days? British soldiers felt as though they were to blame for some of the deaths; felt as though they had contributed to the Jews combined miseries.

CHAPTER 51

The sun had only just arrived upon the horizon on this, the 17th day of April, and the work in the camp grounds was increased from the slow gravity of night work to the full swing of day. The fresh breeze from across the tops of the trees near the forest did little to douse the stench of the dead but the feeling of the wind on the internees' faces gave further assurance that freedom had been handed over to them.

Some of the cleaner barracks, of which were few in the camp, were hastily transformed into makeshift hospitals for the worst of the cases encountered, and other more durable buildings were turned into areas in which the walking sick could be administered.

A sign was erected by the military police at the front entrance of the camp advising that 'dust spreads typhus, 5 mph', a start in the control and eradication of the disease. It was derived that there were in the vicinity of 1,704 'serious' cases of typhus, typhoid and tuberculosis, and many more, milder cases. Lice in the area were rife and this alone contributed to most, if not all, of the typhus outbreaks.

Truckloads of bodies were being removed, the SS visible upon the vehicles, looking sour faced upon the living and then the dead, the mass of bodies, their hard labour stacked miserably where they could be moved once more, into a mass grave, their final resting place.

Some internees were now poking fun at the SS, laughing at them, insulting them. It's all different now that the shoe was on the other foot and the SS and Hungarian guards didn't like it, not one little bit, up to their armpits in death and being ridiculed the way they were, kicks and shoves coming their way, the British unable to restrain the internees' anger at the way in which those bastard SS did deal with their prisoners, how they had degraded human life.

The SS were humiliated time and time again and worked all day, never given time to rest, never given a single moment's solace.

Mass graves: it offered no dignity to be buried in this way, to be shoved into a hole in the ground with thousands of other dead bodies. This was no way for a person to be treated, and so there were still Jews present that thought they were nothing more than mistreated dogs on a leash, but the insanities of the reality evaporated with time and more and more people came to see the situation as it really was. Sanity, after all, was a frame of mind, and only the victim could understand his or her place in society; it wasn't for another to stand up and voice in one clear reflection that this episode of imprisonment could be pushed aside as though it had never happened.

There was no hiding the fragile scars of the mind, there was no speaking of the torture which would be endured each passing day and night as reflection upon the incidents of misery were relived, over and over again. The end was always the same, tears upon the cheek, or a sinking heart that drowned in sheer sorrow and that could never be explained.

CHAPTER 52

A bulldozer was hard at work digging a mass grave, just another reminder of the number of dead, but the death didn't stop there, it continued on for many weeks after liberation.

And a group of some forty Hungarian soldiers were marched along and halted, more than likely those murderous bastards that opened fire a couple of nights before, killing innocents as they tried to escape to meet their liberators as they made their approach towards the camp of pestilence. The Hungarians were being forced to work.

The British guards now guarded the guards; the British guards now kicked the guards; the British guards now hit the guards with the butts of their weapons. Ah, such a beautiful sight to see the arseholes of the world being dealt their just desserts. And amongst the Hungarians and the SS at work were German civilians, forced into helping bury the dead.

A British soldier glanced over to a former SS staff member; saw him handling a body unfitting for the corps. In his eyes he was a guard, SS scum, a bastard of bastards. The officer dashed over to the German and lashed out with a verbal threat.

"Take care of that body, you piece of filth," his German was good; he conveyed his message well. "Mistreat that man and I'll shove my bayonet so far up your arse that you'll be eating it for breakfast."

All the German soldier could do was look down upon the body and look for some semblance, to search for a comparison between it and a human being. To him it was just another Jew, another turd amongst a cesspool of turds. But he found the strength within him to take more care, for he had seen other soldiers of the Third Reich receive the measure of British hospitality to which he had been directly threatened, and he didn't want any of it.

The graves continued to be filled and in the midst of all the work could be seen many German officers, being forced to endure that work which was considered by them to be only fitting for a Jew.

One officer was then seen standing over by a barracks window, fumbling for a cigarette. What guts he did have, what resilience in the face of defeat. A British soldier charged over to him and knocked the hat from upon his head with the end of his rifle and the cigarette fell ungraciously upon the ground. The hat flew through the air and landed on a window ledge and the German was ordered to get back to work by helping move the piles of dead that he had helped create.

The British soldier then saw an innocent face on the other side of the window where the hat had come to rest and as quick as a flash he knocked the hat to the ground, making sure not to touch it with his hands, for anything German placed a foul taste in his mouth. It was a young boy. He then saluted the face to his front, an apology for the disgrace, an apology for disturbing his view, a salute of honour which went to the deserving for having the courage to live through such hell as Bergen-Belsen. The boy saluted back.

A German soldier of the regular army approached the British soldier. He looked from left to right before speaking.

"I can help you," said the German in rather good English.

"What! You filth monger! Get back to work."

"No, listen to me, I know that officer, know him well," said the German soldier. "He is a criminal. I've seen him beat up many poor women in the days leading up to your arrival."

"You don't say," said the British soldier.

"If you can give me some cigarettes, I can tell you who-is-who. My comrades and I have worked hard. It means a lot to get a good meal; you know?"

"Yes... yes, I know," said the British soldier. "Have a look around, you can see for yourself how hard it is to get good food."

"Yes; but this is the SS, not the regular army. We have always treated the prisoners of war with respect. It's the SS, they are the scum," and the soldier spat upon the ground."

"You will come with me," said the British soldier. "I'd like to hear more."

CHAPTER 53

All SS personnel had eben arrested and disarmed, Lieutenant-Colonel Taylor having rewritten the truce in the name of justice. It was about time that a little justice was served back to the SS scum.

The arrests continued as a bulldozer went about its work, but with a mass grave dug it was now turned to the task of burying. Due to the slow progress of burying the dead the bulldozer was now employed in pushing the heaps of dead into the grave, and it wasn't a pretty sight.

Bodies were punctured and ripped about, legs and arms ripped from their sockets, stomachs opened to the air around. It was hard work for the men operating the machinery and rests were awarded frequently, for there wasn't a man amongst them that could handle the torture of bodies being ripped apart for very long, and the stench... it was unbearable.

A bulldozer had to be used, there was no choice in the matter, for the diseased and starved were dying quicker than they could be buried, so work by hand alone was out of the question, at least for a while. If only the British could convince the stubborn internees who failed to trust them that they were there to help.

It wasn't until the first British nurses arrived on the scene that the last of the disbelievers trusted in what was being said: that they were free and liberated.

And it was only then, when a new dish of high-calorie food commenced to be fed to them by the hand of these angels, that they wholly believed that they were free. It was then that the nurses were struck hard by the effects of their tender touch, as the liberators had been affected before them. It was sheer horror for them to see that dozens of men and women were dying from the feeding as they were so unused to good food as opposed to slop.

Giving them food was killing them but they all hoped the new meals would turn the tables and bring good health back to all.

CHAPTER 54

The SS staff of Bergen-Belsen were not provided any leniency. The camp was in its third day of liberation and many of them were being sold out by the German regular army for the price of a meal and a cigarette, which was better than being fed the little they received as murderous prisoners. Justice now began to be metered out as it should; in great quantity.

The SS administration staff, as individuals, were now being pointed out and treated in much respect to the way in which they had treated their prisoners. 'This one was a guard, and so was he'; 'I saw that one on the tower, and that one shooting a prisoner dead'; 'and that one over there, he kicked two poor women to death'. And so the evidence mounted against them.

The SS were already being forced to reside in barracks which had once been lived in by internees, and fed the same rations that the dying were being provided. There was no longer any luxury for these pigs of injustice, where their pride was fed by the misfortune of others a lot weaker than them. This was one reason that many SS contracted typhus, and many died with the passing of time, but no one cared; why should they? The regular soldiers weren't treated nearly as badly, for the average British soldier understood, quite clearly, who lay at fault in this dreadful debacle. But now, after the finger-pointing had started, the SS were dealt a more severe blow.

Two SS staff, having performed duties as guards at one time or another, being accused by the internees, were soon set up and thrown into a barrack with many internees, and the internees dealt out their own justice by kicking and punching. It took some time before the two bodies were thrown out of the barrack, dead and with grimaces of pain and suffering written upon their faces.

It was no surprise to see that many of the SS were either shot or worked to death, or bludgeoned by the heavy hand of a sergeant on duty.

The bunker had been cleared of the few internees that had been deprived of their freedom, and others still that had been deprived of life, but it was a shame to see the bunker going to waste and so it was employed well as a place in which to maintain some control over those SS that had been pointed out to the British as being heinous and criminally unjust.

CHAPTER 55

The British sergeant was furious to say the least, for the interrogation should have been completed already, but he held his tongue and was gentleman enough not to allow the men under his charge see how displeased he was with the young officer's inability to carry out his duty.

These damn SS shouldn't be getting off so easily. Not three days ago there were three women found in the bunker; two of them were dead and another was barely alive – the men detained in the bunker were no better off.

"We carried out an interrogation this morning," advised the captain as the unbolted door was pulled open. "We couldn't get much out of them. They're not very pretty to look at, I'm afraid."

"The slime on one boot looks much the same as the other, sir," replied the sergeant as he entered the cell. "Now get up! Come on! Hurry up!" yelled the sergeant as he hit out with the metal rod in his hand, poking one of the half dozen SS as he got up off the stone floor. "Get on your feet, you dirty bastard!"

"Is there anything else, sergeant?" asked the captain.

"No, thank you, sir," replied the sergeant. "I'll take care of them from here, thank you very much."

"Yes, well I'll leave you to it then," and the captain removed himself from the corridor.

The SS had blood pasted all down their fronts and the looks in their eyes were those displayed by the defeated. One of the guards was trembling and looked the sergeant in the eye as best he could.

"Why don't you just kill us instead of tormenting us like this? We don't deserve this. We are men," said the SS bastard. "I can't take it anymore; the beatings, this stinking punishment. Just kill me and be done with it."

The MP beside the sergeant whispered to him then, "He's been saying that damn same thing, over and over again. He was doing it this morning when we came in to give him his just dessert."

"Well, you've done a good job," said the sergeant as he looked down again upon the SS filth. "Now get up, you filthy dogs; MOVE IT!"

CHAPTER 56

An order was delivered to all of the British. There were to be no more beatings, no more open-handed punishment of the SS; it was against the Geneva Convention; and so if punishment was to be delivered it was to be done behind closed doors. And so, to the dissatisfaction of the internees, the beatings were seen to be discontinued.

The SS that remained, along with the others of the German contingent, had now been awarded freer rein upon the way in which they handled the dead and from that moment on became more careless in every task they performed.

Too hard it was to get a filthy, stinking Nazi, by himself. And the women guards were just as bad; filthy swines, easily mistaken for men as their loud mouths could attest. There wasn't a lady amongst the group of scum thought mistakenly as female; it was a joke amongst some of the British that to have sex with one would be like taking a razor to your own genitals: what pleasure was there in that? How could any man, German or not, seek pleasure with one so outwardly hostile and vicious? Ugly was too good a word to use on them. Their snarls were like that of a rabid dog, and that was when they were smiling. And so to work they were forced, to endure the same as the men, to be forced amongst the dead and told to clean up their mess.

The SS women guards did as they were ordered, but worked as slowly as they dared, and as the bodies were handled, being thrown into the large graves, one of them looked up and smiled. She was happy and content to see so many dead, happy in her heart that she had helped clean out the Jews of her beloved country. She continued on through the hours of the day, one body after the next thrown into the hole, and still she smiled.

CHAPTER 57

German Regular soldiers were escorted from camp on April 20th, as per the truce that had been signed, but instead of becoming Prisoners of War they were to be returned to their own lines.

They marched off from the Panzer barracks with their weapons with them and for this kind gesture, of allowing them freedom, they sabotaged the water supply to the barracks and hence the evacuation programme. Even in defeat, and being found guilty of crimes against humanity, the Germans were still proud to commit further heinous acts of destruction against the Jews. This was the day that the evacuation process was to commence, the sick to be drawn from the horror camp and placed into real hospital beds; but now, thanks to the scum of the earth, another delay was suffered.

Why on earth did the allies have to be so honourable?

CHAPTER 58

April 21st, and the evacuation commenced in earnest from Bergen-Belsen, the operation now equipped with approximately 7,000 beds and 250 tonnes of medical supplies and equipment. The job was so large that much was needed and confiscated from nearby towns and villages. For the operation to be successful they need 14,000 blankets, 7,000 mattresses, and 5,000 stretchers; the scale of the evacuation was so large that it was said by a high-ranking official that the British should get on with the task at Bergen-Belsen, or continue with the war, but it could not do both; but to the credit of the Union Jack they continued with every task that they were issued.

The internees were transferred to the Panzer barracks which had been transferred into a hospital and transit camp, and here they were treated and cared for, their emancipated bodies lying upon beds and stretchers waiting to be provided medical attention. Here the starved received much care, but time wasn't on the side of the allies and the patients had to be taken care of and moved on once able to be moved, for there were literally thousands dying of all manner of disease. There was also the German Military Hospital which was a part of the infrastructure for the Panzer school, and it didn't take too long for the entire complex and surrounding buildings to be turned into one hell of a huge hospital in which to service the sick from Bergen-Belsen.

The German Military Hospital was to be known as the Glyn Hughes Hospital and it sat in serene surroundings, with 250 brick buildings and five wings attached, and the entire area was adorned with a huge lawn and garden area. Wards on the ground floor opened up to the sports ground where the sight of shrubs, trees, and clock tower, helped promote healing, but the swastika and eagle, so much larger than life it was, wiped the grins from faces as one looked upon the symbol of those scum that had murdered so many. There were sterilising and anaesthetic rooms and a modern operating theatre; kitchens, cellars, store rooms and a room for which to carry out post-mortems. It was spared no expense.

The Panzer Training School was also a great commodity which was taken advantage of. Its grounds were well manicured with lawns, trees and shrubs. Over one hundred two-storeyed buildings existed here which normally housed up to two hundred men apiece, but now, instead of training men for war, it was to be used for healing the sick. Administration buildings, canteens, kitchens, halls, quartermaster stores, workshops; there was even a picture theatre. A swimming pool, heated bath, and showers galore were but simple appendages to this monstrosity of exquisite beauty and convenience. There were also conveniences for the German officers: solarium, banquet halls, ball-room and ante-rooms, all topped off with parquet floors and crystal chandeliers. It was enough to make anyone from Bergen-Belsen sick to the stomach.

CHAPTER 59

The very weak; the very sick; the almost dead. They were left to die. There were so many thousands that needed to be saved and only those with a chance at survival were picked up by the stretcher-bearer parties.

The medical officer was first to enter the building and dozens of hands went up in the air.

"Take me, please, I'm sick," said one.

The doctor looked into her eyes and saw that she was indeed sick and probably would not last long. He saw another and pointed her out to the first stretcher behind him.

"Her; and her as well, quickly now."

"And me, please, I have to see my mother."

"No, not her; that one over there," said the medical officer and on they continued, clearing out those they knew could be saved; many of the others would die.

"My wife," said an elderly man as he was stretchered out. "She's over there, look, you can see for yourself."

The medical officer looked over to see an old woman still upon her bunk and holding dearly to her stomach, and then she wriggled a little and held out her hand.

"I'm sorry, we can't take her."

"But, my wife; please."

"Move along now, come on; next stretcher, quickly please."

This went on for eight hours a day, day in, day out. Move into a hut and take your pick, but pick well, for the weakest would simply drain away the resources.

The stretchers were then carried immediately to the stable where twenty stalls were equipped with hot water and scrubbing brushes. This was the 'human laundry' where each and every one was shaved and cleaned with soap before being dusted down by powder: DDT.

Medical staff would take the soap and brushes and start scrubbing away, the pain of the cleaning being very real. Bed sores and ulcers simply burned with pain. Hair was cut off to the scalp, completely inundated with lice, lice so thick that it was absolutely intolerable and sent internees mad with the pain of scratching their heads till they bled and became infected; where were they when the DDT truck first arrived, but too scared or weak to show themselves, at the back of the barracks and unable to extricate themselves from their bunks: many reasons were evident.

German nurses displayed much displeasure at first in the work that lay ahead of them, laughing and joking about the whole sodden idea of washing the Jews, but as the first batch appeared upon stretchers, and they saw the condition in which the internees were in, they put aside their hatred and acted as good nurses do, working their fingers to the bone and treating the sick as they should be treated. Each worked twelve to fourteen hours a day, every day, and surrendered themselves to the fact that the SS were not as human as they first thought. They won the respect of their British counterparts and of the forty-eight German nurses that worked so hard, thirty-two came down with typhus. The British were advised by the German officer in command of the nurses, that they had already been vaccinated against the disease: he'd openly lied.

From the stable the patients were moved to the hospital and here they underwent the treatments required for their particular situation, which were so very much the same that little difference there was between each.

CHAPTER 60

The process of evacuation had now commenced, on April 24th, at 9:00am precisely. The delay was mainly due to confusion in offering orders, departments unsure as to whose responsibility it was to tend the healthy, for most attended the sick, the needy, those requiring immediate assistance.

Barracks were called out and women lined up. They were loaded onto trucks and taken to the Panzer barracks where they were registered by volunteer clerks, and then to the showers where further dusting was undertaken, hot showers and food for all. It continued all day; every day.

And as the weeks unfolded so the sick and healthy were evacuated back to their homelands, but for many of them, they must remain behind with nowhere to go.

On April 29th, all SS prisoners were escorted to Celle gaol and on May 5th a Russian battalion replaced the Hungarian's on guard duty: so much for the dream of Himmler to have the allies go to war alongside him against the Russians.

On May 15th the Russians at guard duty all departed for repatriation; it had been a long war for them, but even longer for those poor souls, the internees of Bergen-Belsen.

May 18th; 13,834 patients had been admitted to hospital, all having passed through the 'human laundry' in the process, and of deaths that had occurred; only two. By May 19th, the entire camp had been evacuated.

Many thanks must go to the following for their contribution in helping those of Bergen-Belsen:

14th Amplifier Unit
Intelligence Corps
63rd Anti-Tank Regiment, Royal Artillery
10 Garrison
102 Control Section
113 Anti-Aircraft Regiment Royal Artillery
1575 Artillery Platoon RASC

11 Field Ambulance
9 Brigade General Hospital
107 Mobile Laundry
224 Military Government Detachment
618 Military Government Detachment
904 Military Government Detachment
British Red Cross
96 student volunteers from London

The memories of Bergen-Belsen remained with my grandfather all of his life as indicated by some of the last words that parted his lips at the time of his death. Even in the hour of his death he could clearly see the horrors imparted upon the Jews by the Germans.

www.ingramcontent.com/pod-product-compliance
Lightning Source LLC
Chambersburg PA
CBHW032138020426
42334CB00016B/1213